W9-BDV-593

The World of
Butterflies

A Fully Illustrated Guide to These Delicate Jewels of Nature

The World of
Butterflies

A Fully Illustrated Guide to These Delicate Jewels of Nature

Patrick Hook

GRAMERCY

Acknowledgements

I would like to thank the following people from the University of Exeter
for their assistance in providing material for this book:

Rolf Herbert — School of Biological Sciences,
Professor Derek Partridge — School of Engineering & Computer Science,
Dr. Chris Smith — School of Engineering & Computer Science,
Dr. Peter Vukusic — School of Physical Sciences,
Dr. Robin Wootton — School of Biological Sciences

I hope it goes without saying that I would also like to thank the two
photographers who provided the bulk of the pictures, namely Simon
Coombes and Alan Barnes. Simon deserves especial thanks for patiently
following my requests to supply life-cycle sequences, pictures of foodplants,
and so on! I would like to thank Jonathan Watts and Faye Nicholls for
supplying, amongst others, the excellent pictures of butterflies in flight.

Contents

Introduction

This Southern White Admiral (*Ladoga reducta*) looks very similar to the Purple Emperor, to which it is closely related.

Butterflies have captured the attention of mankind since the earliest times, as is evinced in their appearance in paintings and sculptures for thousands of years. Why are they so fascinating? How do they capture our imagination so readily? Some would say that it's their patterns and colors, others that it's a combination of their intricate symmetry and delicate flight. I don't think there is any one answer to the questions, but I do know that anyone who has not been impressed by the spectacular presence of something like a metallic blue morpho in a rain forest clearing needs to check for a pulse!

What are insects?

Insects belong to the phylum Arthropoda — that is they are arthropods. The simple version of this is that they have hard exoskeletons, and pairs of jointed legs. Other members of the class are things like the crustaceans (crabs, lobsters, etc.), arachnids, (spiders, scorpions, etc.) and the centipedes.

Within the phylum Arthropoda is the class Insecta, all members of which have certain distinguishing features: the adults all have six legs, one pair of antennae, and bodies segmented into a head, thorax, and abdomen. Included within the class of insects are cockroaches, beetles, bees, ants, wasps, earwigs, termites, dragonflies, fleas, and, of course, butterflies and moths. There are many others, but they needn't concern us here. It's important to note that while spiders are arthropods, they are not insects. This is easy to establish — they have more than six legs, and their bodies are split into only two major segments.

Butterflies and moths are in the Order Lepidoptera, of which there are somewhere between 150,000 and 170,000 species; something like 20,000 of these are butterflies. No one knows for sure, and never will, as the way the planet is being ruined by deforestation, pollution, and industrialization, so many species are becoming extinct, that we'll never be able to keep up with the losses.

Far Right: Butterflies have six legs as adults; in this picture of a Black Hairstreak (*Strymonidia pruni*) you can see three of them on its left side. You can also see clearly against the white flower the way its "tongue" — the proboscis (here partially uncoiled) — is wound up like a watch spring when not in use.

Right: Appearances can be deceptive — although adult butterflies have six legs, this Owl butterfly only seems to have four! It is a member of the family Nymphalidae, a group of butterflies that is also sometimes known as the "Brush-footed butterflies" or, alternatively, the "Four-footed butterflies." In fact they do have six legs, but two of them are reduced, and often have tufts of scales that make them look like small brushes.

What is the difference between a butterfly and a moth?

This is the magnificent Giant Owl butterfly — (*Caligo memnon*) resting during the day. It is unusual in that it flies during dusk, swooping in and out of the undergrowth in a manner most unlike "normal" butterflies. The eyespots have generated all sorts of explanations as to their intent — some suggest that they mimic an owl's face when the wings are flashed at an enemy, others that they look like a large carnivorous bullfrog when viewed from certain angles.

One of the most common questions any lepidopterist is asked by members of the public concerns the difference between a butterfly and a moth. The question is usually on the lines of "Surely, moths are small brown things that fly at night, and eat clothes, whereas butterflies fly during the day, and are nice pretty things?" Unfortunately, it's not nearly so simple. There are many other misunderstandings too, such as "butterflies hold their wings closed above their heads when they're shut, but flat to the ground when they're open." Well, this is patently not so — look at the picture of a Silver-Spotted Skipper on page 13. To confuse the issue further, many thousands of moth species hold their wings closed above their backs, "just like a butterfly."

Another feature often suggested as a structure to tell the two apart is the antennae — the common perception is that on a butterfly they're clubbed, and on a moth they're furry — but this is wrong again! Many thousands of moth species have antennae "just like a butterfly," and some butterfly species have "moth-like" antennae.

One of the structures that is almost a distinguishing factor, is the *frenulum* — the special "wing-catch" used to keep the hind wings from riding up over the fore wings. In nearly all butterflies it is of one type, and in most moths, it is another. However, there is an Australian skipper called *Euschemon rafflesia* which causes this distinction to fail, as the male has a moth-type frenulum — there are also several moth species which have a butterfly-type wing-catch.

As mentioned earlier, the idea that "butterflies are pretty and fly by day, but moths are dull and brown, and fly by night," is a common sentiment — but it's completely erroneous. Take, for example, the Urania moth illustrated on page 12. If you're looking for a "dull and brown night flyer," you couldn't be more wrong: it's obviously highly colored — and it also flies by day!

The issue of day flying against night flying is certainly not clear-cut at all, as there are a great many moths that are day fliers, although there are very few butterflies that fly at night. There are species that will fly at night during migration while over the sea, but it's not their usual behavior — given the choice they will rest at night.

When an animal is active by day, it is said to be diurnal, and when it is active by night, it is said to be nocturnal. There are, however, countless species that are active in the half-light of dusk and dawn — these species are said to be "crepuscular." Examples of diurnal moths include many of

the Tiger moths, which are often mistaken for butterflies, but there is a family of moths that are nearly all day fliers. These are the Burnet moths (Family Zygaenidae), which — like so many diurnal moths — are chemically protected from the majority of predators. It has been shown that some of them have traces of cyanide within their body tissues.

Although there are very few nocturnal butterflies, there are a great many that are crepuscular, including many of the Satyrs — of the family Satyridae — however, the most impressive are the "Owl" butterflies, of the genus Caligo. These butterflies occur in South America, up through Central America, and into the West Indies. Their larvae mostly feed on banana plants, where they can become pests in commercial plantations. The adults often like to feed on rotting fruit, which can be their downfall, as collectors often use this weakness to set bait-traps for them.

Right: This is not a butterfly at all — it's a brightly colored Urania moth! Many people think that all moths are dull brown things that eat clothes, but they couldn't be more wrong.

Center Right: This is the underside of the same moth, *Urania ripheus*. Like many other butterflies and moths the coloration is just as intricate as on the upper surfaces.

Far Right: The Skipper family causes all sorts of headaches when it comes to the classification of butterfly species, as well as with trying to decide upon a definitive difference between butterflies and moths. This Silver-Spotted Skipper is holding its wings in a manner quite unlike that of most butterflies.

Butterfly classification — How they are named

Most butterflies have an English name, and all have a Latin one, their scientific label which is derived from the "binomial" system which was first used by Carl Linnaeus (properly written Carl Von Linné) in 1753, in his book *Species Plantarum*. This was the starting point for scientific nomenclature for botanists, and the same happened for zoologists when Linnaeus published the tenth edition of *Systema Naturae* in 1758. What made him unique amongst scientists of his time was that he was a very systematic worker — being very thorough and orderly. Can you imagine the mess we'd be in today if Linnaeus had tried to impose a naming system on over a million different animal species without it being rigorous and methodical?

The Latin name has at least two parts, and may well have "extra" names tacked on the end. Sometimes they translate into meaningful phrases, especially those named back in Linnaeus's time. For instance, the Small Blue, is known scientifically as *Cupido minimus*, which translates as "Little Cupid." This is because it is a beautiful little insect, deserving of such a name; this is typical of the period when scientists liked to put a little romance into their work — in this case it was described for science in 1775 by Fuessly.

When the species in question has various subspecies, an addition is made to the name; for instance, when the English form of the Old World Swallowtail, Latin name *Papilio machaon*, is considered, it has the word *britannicus* added, so it becomes *Papilio machaon britannicus*. Notice also that the first letter of the Latin name is spelled with a capital: this is the "generic name," whereas the first letter of the second — the specific name — and any others is lower case.

You will often also see a name and possibly a date at the end of the Latin name, such as "Linnaeus, 1758" — this is the Descriptor — the person who first described the species for science, and the date is when this information was first published. However, if the name and date are placed in parentheses, it means that the species has been moved from the genus where it was first placed into another one. This may all sound a bit complicated, but it's scientific convention — it also helps to clarify the situation if someone else mistakenly uses the same Latin name for a different species.

One of the many confusing aspects of naming any plant or animal is that, as we discover more and more about which species are related to which, we have to reclassify them — that is, we have to take them out of the place where we formerly thought they belonged in the "giant family tree of life," and put them in what we hope is the right place. This means that we have to change their Latin name. To make matters even more confusing, a single species may have many different common names, even in the same country. For instance the Peacock butterfly formerly had the scientific name *Vanessa io*. This then became *Nymphalis io*, and then *Inachis io*. But the Peacock butterfly of Europe is a very different species from that called the Peacock in the United States.

The Small Blue's Latin name *Cupido minimus* translates as "Little Cupid" — a reflection of the romantic esteem in which butterflies were held in the late eighteenth century when it was named.

The evolution of butterflies

The story of butterfly evolution is incomplete; butterflies are inherently so delicate that their remains are very rarely preserved — there are, therefore, many gaps in our knowledge. Insects first made an appearance about 400 million years ago, having evolved from the same ancestral line as the spiders and centipedes. This was back in the Devonian period, in the Paleozoic era. Winged insects made an appearance soon after, somewhere around 50 million years later, during the Carboniferous period. Moths evolved before butterflies, but it is actually very difficult to say when. This is because they developed out of caddis-flies (Order Trichoptera), and there is no single stage where they stopped being caddis-flies, and started being moths. Butterflies evolved about 40 million years later, during the Cretaceous period.

Finding a fossil butterfly is a very rare event — less than 50 have been found to date, including those preserved in amber. The best fossil butterflies have been found at the Florissant Fossil Beds National Monument in central Colorado, which is world-renowned for the quality of its fossils. The beds there produce fossils that are in the order of 35 million years old. The oldest conclusive lepidopteran fossil found, however, was in England at Charmouth. This was a moth called *Archaeolepis mane*, and is from the Lower Jurassic, which makes it about 185 million years old.

The evolution of butterflies was directly linked to that of flowering plants — this is because of mutual interdependence; the butterflies need the flowers to feed on, and the plants need the butterflies to act as pollinators. This is achieved when butterflies travel between flowers to feed — as they do so, they also transfer pollen; this is sometimes so specific that only one species of plant can feed the butterfly, and conversely the butterfly may be the only species that can pollinate the plant. The consequence of this is that if one becomes extinct, so does the other.

Red Admirals can frequently be found in large numbers, as they greedily consume nutritious fruit sugars. Often these have fermented into alcohols by the time the butterflies reach them, resulting in inebriated individuals wobbling about uncertainly!

The butterfly life cycle

1 The eggs of a butterfly when seen up close are very intricately constructed, but the reason why remains a mystery. This is the egg of the Zebra (*Heliconius charitonius*), which has been laid at the end of a tendril to minimize the risk of it being eaten by other caterpillars.

2 This strange looking beast is the larva of the Purple Hairstreak butterfly. You can see how effectively it hides amongst the twigs pretending to be an innocuous leaf bud. Every season countless numbers of caterpillars are found and eaten by predators, but usually enough survive to produce a new generation. The efforts of mankind have, however, put such pressure on the ecosystem that many of the delicately balanced relationships between predator and prey have been upset, resulting in species becoming extinct the world over.

All butterflies and moths go through the same basic life cycle. They start out as eggs (also known as "ova'), and when these hatch, they do so as very small caterpillars, properly known as "larvae." These then go through several stages (or "instars'), each of which is separated by a skin change, known as a "molt," or "ecdysis." When the larva has reached a certain size, it changes into a chrysalis, or "pupa." It stays like this for some time, and then emerges as the adult, or "imago."

The various butterfly families use many different methods of egg-laying. Sometimes they lay them singly, sometimes in batches, on the underside of a leaf. Others choose to lay their eggs on dead leaves or twigs, or on rocks near their foodplant — this is usually to avoid the eggs being eaten by other caterpillars or herbivorous animals. Another way to reduce the risk that the eggs will be eaten is to lay them on a part of the plant that is rarely consumed, such as a tendril.

Some plants have evolved a chemical defense system that will kill any eggs laid on its leaves, before they get a chance to hatch. When this is the case, the butterfly has to lay its eggs nearby, rather than directly onto the foodplant. Perhaps the most unusual place used by a butterfly for egg-laying is in a cobweb — this is done by the Australian Rustic (*Cupha prosope*), from New Guinea and eastern Australia. This might sound a strange place for egg-laying, but what safer location could there be for them than within the striking range of a spider? This species of butterfly continues with the safety theme while it's a small larva, as it dangles on the end of a silken thread when it's not actively feeding. Most larvae get

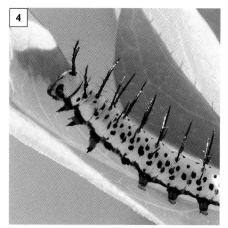  

their first meal after hatching by eating the eggshell — this is often a vital source of protein, which is needed for their arduous struggle through the various instars (an "instar" is the name given to each stage of the larval development between skin changes).

The reason for the larval skin changes is much the same as when a child outgrows its shoes, and needs to change them for a larger size — the caterpillar's skin won't stretch any more, so it's time for a new one! The larva's major preoccupation is with feeding, indeed they have been described as "eating machines," which sums up their role very well. They usually increase their weight many thousands of times in a matter of weeks.

The cuticle, from which the skin is mostly constructed, cannot stretch enough for the expansion in body volume due to the massive food intake, so when it's ready to do so, a hormone is released which triggers the skin to split behind the head; it is then cast off, along with the spiracles, revealing a soft, fresh new one underneath. After a while this hardens up, and the caterpillar wanders off and starts feeding again — in some species though, the caterpillar eats the molted skin first.

When the larva changes into a pupa, it does so in order to rearrange its internal structures, so that it can change into a butterfly. This process, sometimes known as "metamorphosis," is one of the great marvels of the natural world, and has been used as a metaphor throughout history. The Greeks thought that a butterfly's emergence from the pupa was "a personification of the human soul." A thousand years later, in early

3 and 4 This caterpillar of the Zebra butterfly (*Heliconius charitonius*) is busy working its way through a leaf of its foodplant — the passion flower. Notice the spines on its back and sides — these are thought to aid in defence against parasites.

5 You can easily imagine how this Zebra butterfly pupa would blend in if it were among dead leaves.

6 The pupa often changes color just before the adult emerges. This is a result of wing colors showing through the casing.

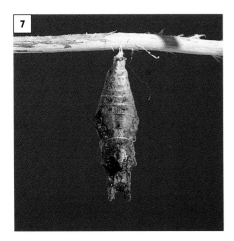

7 Notice how the casing has darkened — this can be a very useful indicator if you want to take pictures of the butterfly's emergence. You can also delay the event by a few hours by moving the pupa to a cool dark place until you are ready. Don't leave it like this for too long though, or it will die.

8 This is the start of the adult Zebra butterfly's emergence. Here, the case has started to split, and the wing colors can just be seen. During this procedure, the butterfly is incredibly vulnerable as its warning coloration is not yet visible to predators.

9 The butterfly has managed to free its head from the pupal case, and is now struggling to extricate its body from the constricting shell.

Christian teachings, metamorphosis was used as a symbol of Christ's resurrection. When the caterpillar is ready to turn into a pupa, it will first find a suitable place for the transformation to take place. With some species this means a short walk to the nearest twig, but with others it may mean a long crawl to a distant location. This is probably to minimize the risk of them being found by parasitic wasps, although clearly the farther apart the members of a brood are, the less is the risk of them falling victim to the same predator.

Once the caterpillar has found a site that meets its criteria, it will anchor itself to the plant, tree, or rock. There are many different anchoring methods, but the most common is the construction of a silken pad, which is glued in some way to the chosen surface. The caterpillar then attaches itself to the pad with a special device called a cremaster, and sometimes also with a "silken girdle," which is just a thin cord running around its middle, to help to support the weight. The final skin change then takes place, in much the same way as a larval molt, although instead of a fresh skin being underneath, the cuticle hardens into a pupal case. The pupa will then wriggle incessantly to make the shed skin break free and drop to the ground. The reason for this is not proven, although it is highly likely that this is to ensure any parasite eggs laid on the skin will be discarded along with it.

In the days leading up to the butterfly's emergence, the pupa will often change color as the wings become visible through the pupal case. This is often accompanied by a lot of "wriggling" around, as it undergoes the final

changes. There is no one set time when emergence occurs in butterflies, but very often they do so in the morning, so that by the time they start to emerge the sun has warmed the air, and the new butterfly can bask in its warming rays. During the time from emergence to first flight, it is extremely vulnerable, as it cannot escape should a predator find it. Until its wings have unfurled, it cannot benefit from any chemical defences it has either, as its warning colors are not visible, and so it may be killed before its unpalatability is discovered.

There is still a great deal of mystery about how butterfly wings go through the transition from being soggy wet "buds" to fully expanded dry wings. The mechanical mechanisms of their unfolding are worthy of research, as there are many places where we could benefit from such perfection of design. For instance, if we could copy this process, it would mean bigger solar panels could be constructed for satellites, as they could be made to fold away more efficiently. This would lower costs, and raise efficiency — in the future, the signal for your mobile 'phone, or television may depend on the engineering of a butterfly wing. The marvels of nature's engineering will still be providing inspiration to mankind for a long time to come!

When the butterfly has dried its wings fully, it will take its first flight. If it's a male, it will spend the first few days of its life as an adult seeking nutrition, looking for flowers rich in nectar from which to extract the all-important sugars that it will use as fuel on its hunt for a mate. This issue is fraught with problems — if the male is too young, he will not be fully

10 Almost there! The wings have now got to be pumped up, and then allowed to dry. The warning colors are not yet fully visible, so this is still a risky time.

11 In the heat of the tropics, it does not take long for the final drying — but the warning colors are already showing, so the most dangerous time is now past.

12 This is an adult Zebra butterfly, showing its distinctive wing markings.

sexually mature, and if the female is too old, she will be infertile, or will already have mated. This is why males typically emerge about a week before the females. It also means that predation will occur mostly among the more common males — in some species the ratio of males to females can be extremely high, with in excess of 50 males for every female. It's therefore important if a butterfly is going to be eaten, that it's a common male, and not a rare female.

Not all butterfly species have male to female ratios this high but, even so, it is not surprising that there is a great deal of competition for fertile females. In some butterfly species, the male will find what he considers to be a good patch of territory, and will patrol it, chasing off any other males that try to encroach. This way, he is proving himself fit to any females that should come his way — if he were not up to the job of defending his territory, he would lose out to a stronger male. There are many other ways that females select their mates: for instance, the "catch me if you can" routine, where she will fly at speed through bushes and trees, and only males that can keep up are considered worthy.

The selection mechanisms and general behavior involved in butterfly reproduction have been the subject of many studies over the years. Some of these have found some very interesting things — for instance, during the 1960s, it was discovered by Stewart Swihart when he was working in Trinidad that early in the day individuals of the Small Postman (*Heliconius erato*) have their vision enhanced in the yellow part of the spectrum. It's believed this is because they feed mostly from yellow flowers. Somewhere around mid-morning, however, something in the brain switches their sight to being predominantly in the red part of the spectrum. This is because the females have distinctive red markings on their wings, which the males use as signals for courtship to begin. They will then inspect anything that is red, and of roughly the right size. When a female makes an appearance, she will be pursued by any males within range. Some things don't change throughout the animal kingdom!

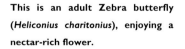
This is an adult Zebra butterfly (*Heliconius charitonius*), enjoying a nectar-rich flower.

Butterflies as pests

A butterfly causing concern in Europe is the Geranium Bronze (*Cacyreus marshalli*), which is in the family Lycaenidae. Originally from South Africa where its larval foodplant was the geranium or pelargonium, somehow it was introduced into Europe, where it is wreaking havoc amongst growers of its foodplant. It is an unusual and attractive butterfly, so its presence won't break the hearts of many lepidopterists — unless they happen to grow geraniums or pelargoniums!

Butterflies and moths can be both pests and instrumental in the control of pests. Mostly they are pests, causing untold amounts of damage to agriculture. The most notorious is, of course, the Cabbage White, which is a general name given to several similar species of Pierids, including the Small White (*Pieris rapae*), the Large White (*Pieris brassicae*), and the Green-veined or Mustard White (*Pieris napi*). Of these three, only the first two are pest species.

Two moths have been instrumental in the control of rogue plant species. These are the Crimson Speckled Footman (*Utetheisa pulchella*), which was used in Australia to bring the Prickly Pear cactus under control. The other is the Cinnabar moth, *Tyria jacobaeae*, which feeds among other things, on ragwort — a poisonous plant found in cattle fields. These represent a serious threat to any animal that eats them. Every year the caterpillars strip the foliage, usually so severely that the plant can't seed.

Probably the most serious lepidopterous agricultural pest is the Gypsy Moth (*Porthetria dispar*), which causes untold economic damage to forested areas. It was introduced to the United States from Europe in 1869 when some were sent to an amateur entomologist in Medford, Massachusetts. Some of these were accidentally allowed to reach the wild, from where they started to colonize the New England states. The moth quickly established itself as there were no natural parasites to limit its spread. This, combined with the fact that each female lays up to a thousand eggs made it a very successful immigrant. Another reason why it has managed to spread throughout the United States is that its larvae will eat many hundreds of different plants, and if its preferred choices are not available, it will eat almost anything.

Many different methods have been tried to wipe out this pest, but none of them has been anything more than a passing success. In the 1960s one of its natural parasites, a braconid wasp (*Rogas indescretus*) was released in yet another attempt. Unfortunately though, it is not limited to the Gypsy moth, and has been found parasitising a related species. This cross-over from pests to the indigenous fauna is a serious problem, and needs to be addressed whenever a non-native parasite or predator is introduced to a new locality.

Other control methods tried include pesticides, diseases, pheromone traps, and encouraging natural predators. Of these, only the traps are ecologically sound, with no impact on other species. Controling pests without damaging the local habitat is a real problem — sometimes releasing infertile males works, and other times parasitic nematode worms will drastically reduce numbers. The answer probably lies with more research, but that suffers from the opposite problem — survival in a harsh economic climate severely limits the number of research scientists!

Predators and parasites

There are many things that prey on butterflies, but none of them do so in a more horrendous manner than some of the parasites. The larva of Tachinidae flies, for instance, feed on living flesh, being internal parasites of various insects and arthropods. The adults of these thick-set bristly flies usually lay their eggs on the skin of their victim, but sometimes use an "egg laying needle" called an "ovipositor" to break the skin so that they can lay their eggs directly into the flesh of the unfortunate individual. Some species lay their eggs onto a likely plant, and the larvae then hatch and wait for a butterfly larva to wander by — they then attach themselves to its skin, and bore through into the flesh. Another method used is to lay very small eggs on the leaves of the foodplant — when the larval victim eats them, the eggs hatch, and the fly larvae bore their way through the gut-wall and into the flesh beyond.

The majority of butterfly parasites though are wasps — albeit very specialized ones. Wasps are members of the Order Hymenoptera, which includes bees and ants. There are three main types of wasp parasites of butterflies, the Braconids (family Braconidae), the Chalcids (superfamily Chalcidoidea), and the most notorious of all, the Ichneumon wasps (family Ichneumonidae).

Once a butterfly has been parasitized, its death is certain, and this can be of tremendous use in the control of pests, such as the Cabbage White. The problem is that where parasites are used as a control mechanism in a new environment, a great deal of research has to be performed first to ensure that they do not "spread over" and destroy other species of butterfly as well.

In one study conducted in the 1930s, it was found that well over 80 percent of Large White (*Pieris brassica*) larvae in the wild had been parasitized by the Braconid wasp *Apanteles glomeratus*. When the female wasp finds a suitable host larva, it lays up to a hundred eggs within its flesh. These then hatch out, and the grubs eat away at the non-vital tissues of the caterpillar. It survives until just before it is due to turn into a pupa, when it dies. The wasp grubs then bore their way out, and pupate in a mass of small yellow cocoons.

Chalcid wasps seem to prefer to parasitize moths, for there seem to be fewer records of them selecting butterflies as their host "victims." This is probably just a lack of knowledge on our part, as it is highly likely that they do indeed range more widely than we realize. The adults of the larger species of Chalcid wasps lay numerous eggs directly into the pupae of

Many wasps feed their young on insect flesh — if you consider that a wasp nest may consist of over 20,000 individuals, and each of them has been fed on insect protein during their "upbringing," a large number of butterflies and caterpillars died to achieve it.

their hosts, but the smaller ones lay their eggs into the eggs of butterflies and moths (among other things). Both are then assured of a certain death. These species of wasps can be very small, sometimes being less than a hundredth of an inch long!

The parasitic wasps are solitary — that is they do not form social colonies: however, there are many truly social wasps, all of which belong to the subfamily Vespinae. Whilst these do not parasitize any butterflies, they do take a huge toll on their numbers every year. Mostly this is due to the wasps hunting down caterpillars and taking them back to the nest, where they are fed to the wasp grubs. If you consider that a wasp nest may consist of over 20,000 individuals, and each of them has been fed on insect protein during their "upbringing," a large number of butterflies and caterpillars died to achieve it. One of the most voracious hunters of insects is the hornet, another social wasp that looks similar to, but is much bigger than, the common wasp.

Another flying insect that preys extensively on butterflies is the robber fly, which belongs to the family Asilidae. The adults of some of the species in this family are active hunters, searching out and killing their prey, whilst others are "ambushers," lying in wait for their victims. The larvae of these flies feed on decaying matter, and so it is only the adults that represent a threat to butterflies.

The list of other animals that prey on butterflies is endless, but the most obvious ones are birds, and to a much lesser extent, bats. This is because most insectivorous bats fly at night, and so take a huge toll on nocturnal moths, whereas day-flying butterflies and moths escape their attentions. Those that fly in the dusk and dawn, however, may well fall victim to these highly adapted predators.

Some of the animals that eat butterflies and moths are not as obvious as birds. For instance, mice take a lot of larvae and pupae, as do lizards and many other animals. However, probably the main predator of butterflies is the spider; these are highly effective hunters, using many different methods to take their prey. The best known method is of course, the web, seen on vegetation the world over. However, some use holes to hide in, and then pounce out on passers-by, whereas others are active hunters searching through the undergrowth for potential meals.

Another highly effective predator of butterflies is the dragonfly. These evolved early on in the history of insect life, well before butterflies first existed. Many of the fossils that have been found demonstrate that some

Main Picture: Lizards are very fond of eating many insects, including caterpillars and butterflies. This one is sunning itself on a rock — this is to keep its body temperature high; as reptiles are cold-blooded, they cannot move fast enough to catch their prey until they are warm.

Inset, Top: The diet of voles is mostly vegetable matter of one sort or another, but they will readily extend this to include caterpillars, pupae, or butterflies given the opportunity.

Inset, Center: Adult dragonflies are voracious hunters of almost all flying insects. This one has found a perch from where it will maintain a lookout for potential victims. They are only predators of butterflies while they are adults, as their larvae live in water, being voracious hunters of many forms of aquatic life.

Inset, Bottom: Wasps are usually opportunists, often taking vegetable matter as well as animal flesh.

primitive dragonflies were very big — over two feet from wing tip to wing tip! Presumably they were able to grow to this size as birds had not evolved to pose a threat to them. Dragonflies are in the Order Odonata — they have two pairs of wings, large compound eyes, and long slender bodies. They are only predators of butterflies in the adult stage, as their larvae live in water, being voracious hunters of many forms of aquatic life.

The biggest killers of butterflies are, however, much smaller than those mentioned above. Fungal infections, bacteria, and viruses without a doubt are the greatest limiting factor to the numbers of butterflies and moths in the natural world. When I say "natural world" I deliberately mean to leave out human intervention, because who knows what mankind will eventually do to the global ecosystem?

When a female butterfly is looking for a suitable foodplant on which to lay her eggs, one of the things she is unconsciously doing is rejecting plants which are too damp for her offspring to stand a reasonable chance of surviving. This is because in damp conditions fungi can prosper, and will kill larvae very quickly. If you are looking for caterpillars in the wild in a temperate climate, you can use this knowledge to your advantage — you can almost forget about searching areas that do not receive enough sunshine to dry out properly. In practice this means, for example, that a north-facing hedge or bank will have very few caterpillars present, whereas a sunlit place may be very productive.

When keeping butterflies in captivity, the biggest threat to their survival is likely to be from bacteria and viruses, along with fungal problems. The only way to guard against this is to keep your cages spotlessly clean, and to disinfect them on a regular basis. It is also a good idea if you construct your cages in the most economical manner possible: you can then afford not to reuse them, which will minimize the chances of them harboring such diseases and infections.

If you examine closely a butterfly that has been caught in the wild, you may well see mites clinging to a leg, an antenna, or around the proboscis. Sometimes the poor butterfly is literally teeming with these tiny creatures. They are, however, not parasites, but are "hitching a ride" to another flower. They don't fly themselves, so they use the butterfly for free transportation — so much for the adage, "there's no free ride"!

Spiders are in the Order Aracneae, of which there are something like 30,000 recognized species throughout the world. They differ from insects in many ways, but the most obvious features are that spiders have eight legs, and their bodies are divided into two major segments. Apart from when it is in its very earliest stages, a spider can be a severe danger to caterpillars and butterflies throughout their life cycles.

The history of the study of butterflies

What was mankind's first interest in insects? Well, of course, no one knows for sure, but some shrewd guesses could be made. My suggestion is that there would have been two major reasons for cavemen to take an interest — firstly, "What do they taste like?" and secondly, "Can they hurt me?"

It would have been many tens of thousands of years before this attitude changed very much. I would suggest that the next reason for early man to take a fresh look at insects would be for providing cordage, especially for bowstrings. This may surprise you, but it is a fact that cave men used weapons to feed and defend themselves, and good tools need bindings, and bows need strings.

As this is well before recorded history began, no one knows when it first happened, but the construction of a good bow requires a good drawstring. Basically there were two sources of material available — those derived from animals, and those from plants. Plant fibres can be excellent, such as those from hemp and flax. Animal-derived strings include gut, sinew, and the one of interest to us here — silk. A good silk drawstring will far outperform gut and sinew, and will cast an arrow in a highly efficient manner. In the 1400s, the book *Le Livre du Roi Modus* says "The string should be made of silk, and nothing else . . . because . . . it will drive an arrow . . . farther than any string made of flax or hemp."

It is an interesting fact that many archers from early history used silk, whereas these days linen will outperform it. Why should this be? Well it's possible that, at that time, the silk from a different species of silk moth was used for drawstrings from that used for making cloth. Any knowledge we had about this has been lost, but the possibility lends credence to the idea that early man knew which silk moths produced the best silk.

Tradition has it that "sericulture," or the study of silk production, started in China somewhere around 2640 BC. Chinese legend has it that an Emperor's wife, one Si-Ling-Chi, discovered the secret in the imperial gardens. The Emperor was so impressed with a silken gown she made, that he created the world's first silk factory.

Personally, while I like reading about myths and legends, I think that the origin of silk production goes back much further than this. Finding materials from which it is possible to make threads is a major preoccupation for anyone trying to survive in the wild. Fisherman from the Trobriand Islands near New Guinea have been using spider webs to make simple fish-traps for a very long time, and I see no reason why it should not date back tens of thousands of years. If this is the case or not, I sus-

It is unclear where the name "butterfly" came from — originally if an insect flew, it was simply called a "fly." The term may have been derived from the yellow Brimstone butterfly, which appears very early in the spring, and was known as the "butter-colored fly."

Above Right: In the summer and early part of the autumn, the Red Admiral is often found feeding from a variety of flowers.

Below Right: The Purple Hairstreak (Quercusia quercus).

pect that the ingenuity of early man would not have taken long to discover the thread-making capabilities of wild silk moths.

I'm sure that this view is guaranteed to upset many archaeologists, as there is absolutely no evidence to support it. However, biologists today are still being surprised by the intimate knowledge of the natural world displayed by the few "primitive" civilizations that haven't had their culture completely destroyed by modern man. An excellent example of this is with the Pygmy Bushmen of the Kalahari Desert in South Africa, who know so much about the minute details of every beetle, every fly, and every moth, that I find it unbelievable that they would have missed the thread-making potential of cocoons, had they occurred in their lands. It is a tragedy that so many of these peoples have been wiped out by the influx of modern man throughout the world. Along with their unique cultures and lifestyles, so much knowledge has been lost that will never again be rediscovered.

Whoever it was that first cultivated the silkworm, it has been selectively bred by man for so long now that the caterpillars will not wander away from their food any more, and will starve to death if it (mulberry) is placed even a few inches away. This is the product of thousands of years of human culturing, and was done to make them easy to keep on open trays. They are now so far from their ancestral form that we don't even know what the original moth looked like!

When we move into historical times, we can begin to see a direct interest in the insects themselves. For instance there is a 4,000-year-old Egyptian papyrus which gives details on how to get rid of "lice, fleas, and wasps." The oldest surviving pictures of butterflies are in early Chinese and Egyptian paintings, such as the famous 3,500-year-old fresco from the tomb of Nebamum in Thebes, known as "Fowling In The Marshes." This shows seven beautifully illustrated specimens of the Plain Tiger (*Danaus chrysippus*).

Over the next 2,000 years there was not much advancement in the documentation of natural history. Virgil imagined that "a swarm of honey bees might be generated from a piece of putrid flesh," and Pliny the Younger thought that "many caterpillars have their birth, or being, from a dew that in the spring falls upon the leaves of trees."

In the Dark Ages, butterflies started to make an appearance as decoration in the borders of illuminated manuscripts. Sometimes they were recognizable as actual species, but more often they were composites of several different butterflies that the artists had seen.

The Middle Ages were a time of superstition; in Europe many

believed that butterflies were the souls of living things, and if a butterfly was seen hovering over a cornfield, it was thought to be a bad omen for the crop. Any actual observation was kept to an absolute minimum — for instance St. Thomas Aquinas's tutor believed that caterpillars and butterflies were unrelated.

In a small town in southern Italy, however, it was thought that butterflies were incarnations of the devil. At the same time of year, in the middle of summer, the people would wake to find the town covered in drops of blood, and there would be butterflies all over the place. The locals deduced that they were the work of the devil but the priest was not convinced, and decided to examine things for himself. He discovered that wherever there was a drop of "blood," above it there was also an empty pupal case. Eventually he witnessed a late emergence, and announced to the surprised townsfolk that the blood was nothing more than a natural fluid. This is the first documented evidence of true scientific observation in the history of lepidoptery.

Not much changed until the advent of the microscope, a breakthrough for science — even Galileo (1564–1642) was drawn to the wonders of the natural world, saying "With infinite wonder I have examined very many minute creatures among which the most horrible are the fleas, and the most beautiful ants and moths."

A Dutchman called Jacob Swammerdam (1637–80) discovered by dissection that "the skins of the caterpillar and the chrysalis are enveloped in each other, as is also the butterfly with all its organs, but these in a fluid stage." He published his findings in his book *Historia Insectorum Generalis* in 1669, but as no one believed him, he was thoroughly discredited.

Maria Sibylla Merian (1647-1717) was the first person to have her observations of metamorphosis recognized. She was one of the foremost wildlife artists of her time and, until recently, was thought to be more or less just that; however, attention was drawn to several of her manuscripts which were in the Library of the Academy of Sciences in Leningrad. These revealed that she was as much a scientist as an artist.

Maria's art tuition started when she was very young — her natural father died when she was only three, and her mother later married a painter, who recognized Maria's potential talent, and fostered it. She grew up in Germany, in the town of Frankfurt-am-Main. By the age of 13, with her study of the silkworm (*Bombyx mori*) she had established a style of painting that she would develop throughout her remarkable life. The fact that she worked from her own observations meant that she was becoming a scientist even then.

She was an amazing lady, not only as an artist-scientist, but later when she was living in Holland, she managed to persuade the Dutch government to sponsor a trip to Surinam to paint tropical animals and plants from life. She did this at 52, when such a journey would have been harsh and hazardous for someone half her age. When she returned, the quality of her work ensured her a place in history.

Another great scientist, Robert Hooke (1635–1703), who was among other things a professor of geometry, an astronomer, and an architect, is considered by many to be the founding father of modern physics. His relevance in the context of butterflies is that he was one of the first to use a microscope for biological research; this, combined with his outstanding talent as an artist, made him one of the great microscopists of his era. He published *Micrographia* in 1665, in which he illustrated a single lepidopterous specimen, which he called "The White Feather-winged Moth," although today it is known as the White Plume moth (*Pterophorus pentadactyla*).

While Robert Hooke's excellent artistry was unusual in the 17th century, over the next hundred years many beautiful works were published, such as *One Hundred and Twenty Copperplates of English Moths and Butterflies*, written by Benjamin Wilkes and published in 1773 (this first appeared as *The English Moths and Butterflies* in 1749). Some of these books showed such good attention to detail, that it is obvious that they must have reared the subjects through from egg to adult, recording each stage as they did so. This is when modern biology really became established, although at the same time it was still fashionable for wealthy gentlemen to collect cabinets of curios in a haphazard and most unscientific manner.

This "cabinet-collecting" was mainly due to the innumerable explorations being made around the world at the time, when it became an integral part of fashionable society to show off curiosities brought from far-flung corners of the earth. In the early days it was considered enough merely to have strange objects on show, but as the collections grew, so did an interest in the science behind them.

It was during this period that Carl Linnaeus established himself as one of the most significant scientists of all time — he set up binomial nomenclature with the publication of the tenth edition of his work *Systema Naturae*, on January 1, 1758. The reason that we use Latin names to this day is because it's the language Linnaeus wr.ote his books in.

At the close of the 18th century 1,147 species of butterflies and moths were known to Fabricius (one of the famous entomologists of the time) — clearly, lepidoptery had become established, and the scene was set for the 19th century to capitalize on this foundational knowledge. That it did so is an understatement. Collecting became an obsession, with vast sums being spent by some to amass huge numbers of specimens — particularly by those rich enough to send professional collectors off to exotic locations in search of the most prized treasures of all — species new to science.

By the mid-Victorian era, the scientific community was well established, and had started to take off. Academia, however, was still held back by the grip of religion — it was still dogma that the world was created in 4004 BC! This perspective received a mortal blow when Charles Darwin finally published *The Origin Of Species* in 1859. He had written it years before, but was worried about being ostracized from his circle of scientific study, and hence did not dare publish until persuaded to do by some of his eminent friends. They were worried that Alfred Russel Wallace would get his work on the same subject in print before Darwin if things were not "hurried along."

Wallace was one of the great collector-naturalists, along with Henry Bates who also traveled widely — he discovered something like 8,000 plants and animals new to science in the space of ten years! Over the course of the 19th century, the number of known species of butterflies and moths had risen tenfold, and lepidoptery had moved from the premises of rich eccentrics into being a fully-fledged science.

The 20th century brought with it several advances, and lots of setbacks. Many of the adventurer-scientists so notorious in the Victorian era were killed in World War I, a needless slaughter that ripped the heart out of an entire generation. This brought with it the collapse of the tradition of patronage by wealthy gentlemen, so expeditions to foreign lands had to be financially justified in other ways — often the work was done by army officers and colonialists who were abroad for professional reasons, and who studied butterflies as amateurs.

Over this period, an enormous amount of scientific work was carried out into every possible aspect of butterfly biology by the increasing number of institutions, universities and research establishments. This invaluable work is continuing to this day, and advances in technology, particularly the use of computerized techniques is allowing detailed modeling of complex systems, such as the interactions of air vortices and insect wings. In the next section, I shall examine this further.

Above Left: The Small Copper (Lycaena phlaeas).

Below Left: The Long-Tailed Blue (Lampides boeticus).

Current scientific research

As I am doing my doctorate at the University of Exeter, in southwestern England, I decided to illustrate the subject of modern scientific work involving butterflies by highlighting three research projects that are currently underway on our campus. Although all three are doing research involving insects, rather surprisingly only one of them is in a biology department! This is on the computer-modeling of insect wings. Closely related to it is the study into the material properties of insect wings — though this project is being conducted in the materials section of the engineering department. The third is in the physics department, where they are studying the mechanisms that create the dramatic iridescent colors of some butterflies.

Right: The complexities of butterfly flight mechanics are a long way from being fully understood. This picture of a skipper butterfly shows well the way that the wings distort in flight — at this instant they are on the "upstroke."

Far Right: This Comma butterfly is flying more or less upside-down — the view we have here is of the upper sides of its wings! Aerial somersaults are very common in many species.

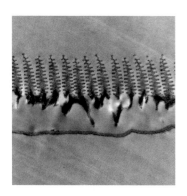

Above: This is a cross-section through a wing scale from a Blue Morpho (*Morpho rhetenor*), as seen through a transmission electron microscope. Each of the "Christmas tree" shapes is a slice through one of the ridges that runs along the scale – they are about 600 nanometres apart. The distances between the "branches," the thickness of the layers, and the space of the air gap that separates them determines the color that is produced.

Right: Dr. Peter Vukusic sets the position of the wing scale — the safety glasses are needed because laser beams can be very dangerous.

Inset: The wing scale has had a red light directed at it, making it produce a red "starburst."

The iridescence of butterfly wings

This research project is being conducted by Dr. Peter Vukusic and Professor Roy Sambles, in the Thin Film Photonics group of the School of Physics, at the University of Exeter.

Over the years, many people have put forward ideas as to how the spectacular colors found on some butterfly wings were produced. Until recently though, no one knew for sure. Some thought it was via liquid crystals, but this has recently been proved to be incorrect. Research such as that being performed here at the University of Exeter has found that the iridescence seen on the wings of certain species of butterflies is entirely structural in origin, and is a produced by a series of thin-film multi-layers.

The natural choices when it came to selecting species to study were, of course, the remarkable Morpho butterflies with their spectacular metallic blue coloration. These come from tropical South America, where they are well known for the vivid flashes created every time the sun catches their wings as they fly through the rain forests.

Several species were studied in detail, using various analytical techniques, including scanning electron microscopes, and specialized laser spectroscopy. It was found that the surface of the iridescent color-producing scales consists of a series of longitudinal ridges, each of which contains a multi-layer structure. If you examine the transmission electron micrograph images of the cross-sections of butterfly wing scales, you see that, when viewed end-on, the multi-layers form Christmas tree-like structures. These multi-layer structures cause selective interference, which then forms the deep blue iridescent color of the Morpho wing.

In order to study the colors further, single scales measuring 0.004-0.008in (0.1mm x 0.2mm), were isolated and mounted on the tips of special needles. These were then placed in the path of a monochromatic light source, which allowed "wavelength-dependent absolute reflectivity spectra" to be recorded for these single scales. If you want to know more about this, you can access the web-site listed at the end of the book.

Characterizing materials in insect wings

Dr. Chris Smith and Professor Ken Evans of the University of Exeter School of Engineering and Computer Science, and Dr. Robin Wootton of the School of Biological Sciences, are working on a project to characterize the materials that make up insect wings. From their perspective, these are small, lightweight aerofoils which differ from those of aircraft in that they have vastly different operating conditions. While a great deal of work

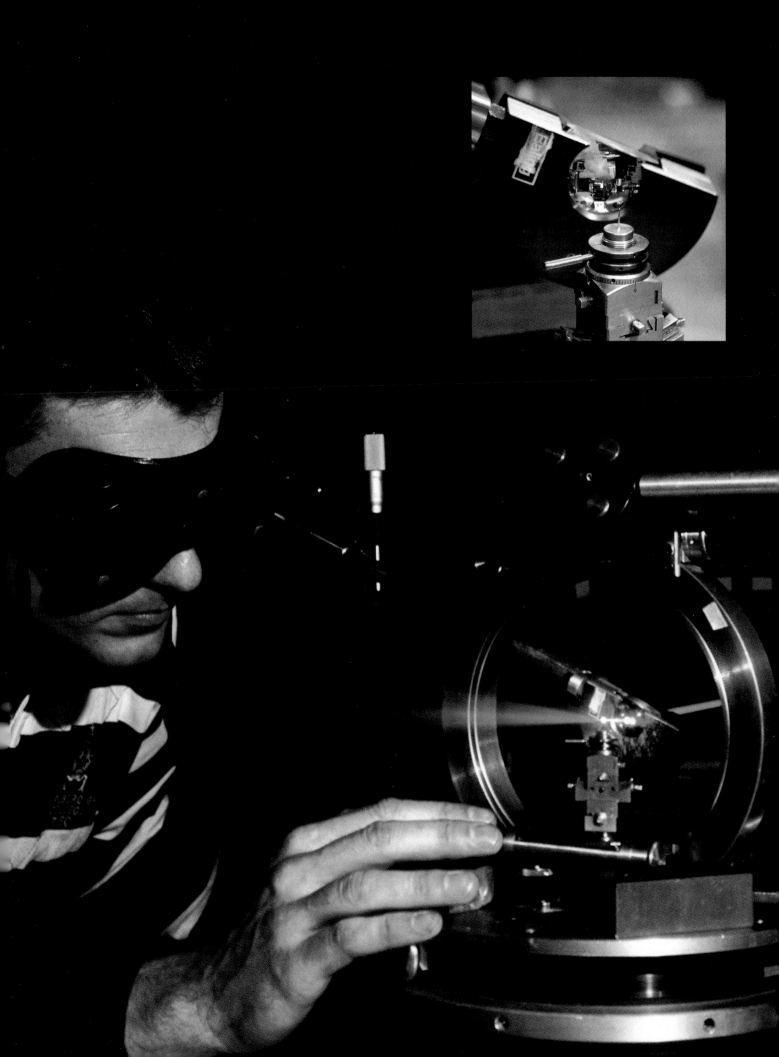

1 This is the layout of the wing veins of the Tobacco hornworm (*Manduca sexta*). Their geometry and dimensions are used to construct a "virtual" wing (computer model), on which loads are then imposed.

2 Here, the simulated wing has been subjected to two theoretical loads, one from above, the other from below. The areas in red show the highest stress concentrations — demonstrating that if the wing was loaded like this, it would snap fairly quickly.

3 Here, the simulated wing has been subjected to two theoretical loads, but this time both are from above — resulting in the deformation shown. As before, the red areas show the highest stress. The fact that the wing is mostly yellow and orange (medium stress) demonstrates that this is much closer to the type of loading that it was "designed" for than in 2.

has been put into studying the wings of aircraft, very little is known about the mechanical behavior of insect wings.

It's obvious that wings are vitally important to flying insects, therefore as far as these scientists are concerned, to understand the insects, first you need to understand their wings. From an engineer's point of view, you need to know their material properties — but the problem is that conventional characterization techniques don't work very well with the very small material specimens that you obtain from things like butterfly wings.

To get around this, Chris has built a novel piece of equipment which is probably the "smallest" materials' testing machine in the world. By this I mean that it will test very small samples — for instance, it can accurately measure the tensile strength of a piece of butterfly wing less than 40 thousandths of an inch (1mm) across. When operating, this machine applies a deformation to the test specimen, and then measures the resultant forces. It can work accurately at displacements of a quarter of a millionth of an inch! Using this and other techniques, it is hoped that a full picture of the material properties of insect wings will be built up. This work is providing invaluable information for another research project being done on the same university campus, this time over in the School of Biological Sciences.

Finite element modeling of insect wings

Rolf Herbert and Dr. Robin Wootton of the School of Biological Sciences are working to produce a computer model of the way that insect wings deform under load. The reasoning behind this project is that even though our knowledge of insect wings is impressive, little is known about their structural engineering. This is Rolf's doctoral research project, where he is using rigorous structural analysis to gain an understanding of why insect wings are designed as they are.

He and Robin are using "finite element modeling," which is one of the latest computerized techniques for mechanical analysis. Basically, a finite element model combines material properties like Young's modulus, with structural information, like the shape of the veins, to produce a complex virtual structure. Realistic loads can then be applied, and the resulting deformations and stresses recorded and viewed.

The initial investigations are being carried out using a moth — the Tobacco Hornworm (*Manduca sexta*), which is an American hawkmoth. This is because it is a species that is commonly used for scientific work on wings, and is therefore the insect whose flight mechanics and physiology are best understood.

The tubular veins of Manduca wings are mostly less than 0.012in (0.3mm) in diameter, and the membrane itself is on average only two microns in thickness. This is where this study interfaces with that mentioned previously concerning "Characterizing materials in insect wings" — the information from the micro-materials testing machine they developed can be used to provide vital data for the finite element model.

Once the material properties have been established, they must be combined with accurate geometric data. This is then used to build up the elements that go together to form the insect's wing — the FEM software is then used to start forming a picture of its deformation characteristics. Eventually, they hope to be able to model the entire flight process, but as it's a tremendously complex process, it will be a long time coming!

These projects at the University of Exeter are just three examples of work that is being performed all over the world. Some people may question the justification for performing basic research like this, but without it human knowledge would stagnate — and for those of us driven by the desire to learn, that would be a catastrophe!

4 Here, the simulated wing has been subjected to a single theoretical load. The large amount of blue (low stress) shows that of the three, this produces the lowest stress concentrations. It is clearly in the interests of butterflies if their wings are kept as light as possible — it reduces their inertia (increasing the rate at which they can be accelerated), and minimizes the energy required for flight.

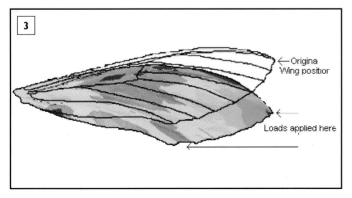

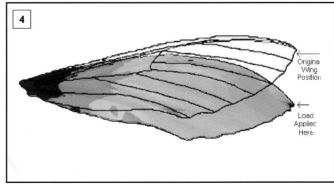

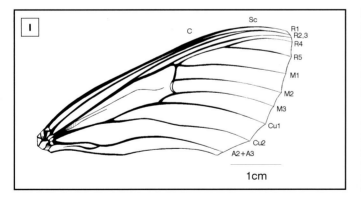

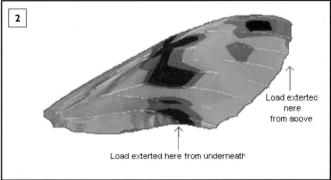

Coloration

The Monarch is one of the widest-ranging butterflies in the world – there are very few countrie where it, or one of its close relatives does not occur. Its bright warning colors show that it is evil-tasting: as a larva, it synthesizes poisons from its food-plant, the Milkweed (*Asclepias*). These toxins are carried forward through the pupal stage, and eventually into the adult. Because of this the Monarch has many mimics. (See next page.)

Coloration is vitally important to all butterflies — if they have the wrong colors, they are either likely to get eaten by predators, or they'll fail to attract a mate of the right species. They have, therefore, evolved a complex series of mechanisms to ensure that their chances of surviving and successfully attracting the right mate are optimized.

The simplest of these to understand is camouflage — if they can hide from predators, they are much less likely to get eaten. There are a variety of ways to use camouflage, but they all use deception of one form or another. If you can convince a predator that you're a dead leaf, they're not going to be interested in eating you! The Indian Leaf butterfly is a past master at achieving this — when Alfred Russel Wallace, who was one of Darwin's contemporaries, was trying to catch one, he wrote this in *The Malay Archipelago*:

"This species was not uncommon in dry woods and thickets, and I often endeavoured to capture it without success; for after flying a short distance, it would enter a bush among dry or dead leaves, and however carefully I crept up to the spot, I could never see it till it would suddenly start out again, and then disappear in a similar place. At length I was fortunate enough to see the exact spot where the butterfly settled; and though I lost sight of it for some time, I at length discovered that it was right before my eyes, but that in its position of repose it so closely resembled a dead leaf attached to a twig as almost certainly to deceive the eye even when gazing fully on it."

Likewise, other species use deception to full effect by pretending to be anything from a piece of tree bark to a bird dropping! A totally different form of deception, however, is to pretend to be a different, but poisonous species. This is called Batesian mimicry. There are many butterflies that are highly distasteful to most predators — a classic example of which is the Monarch. As a larva, it synthesizes poisons from its foodplant, the Milkweed (*Asclepias*). These toxins are carried forward through the pupal stage, and eventually into the adult.

The poisons extracted from the foodplant are quite complicated, and are known as "cardiac glycosides," or "cardenolides'; these cause birds that ingest it to be violently ill, inducing vomiting and general distress for about half an hour. It's worth noting that it's not in the interests of the butterfly species for the poison to be fatal, as it's better to have the predator survive with the knowledge that the warning colors are there for

rhetenor
helena. Stgr.

Above: The wing scales which produce the iridescent effect of these Morpho butterflies represent the pinnacle of butterfly coloration.

Below Right: Bright colors on an insect usually warn of their unpalatability — this Garden Tiger moth (*Arctia caja*) is another demonstration that it's not only butterflies that can have beautiful colors and markings.

Far Right: For many years, this butterfly *Danaus (Salatura) genutia* was given the same Latin name as the Monarch (*Danaus plexippus*). It is now, however, recognized as a close relation, rather than the same species.

a very good reason, than it is for it to die and be replaced by another one that needs to learn the lesson all over again.

This chemical protection is therefore broadcasted via the color scheme to warn of its unpalatability. Hence, when a bird sees the colors, it knows that if it eats the butterfly, it is likely to be very sick. We haven't found out yet just how this is achieved — it's either that, when young, they try eating insects with warning coloration, and soon learn that things with bright colors are distasteful, or there may be some instinctive response. That is, they may inherit a dislike of warning colorations. The learning process has often been observed with monkeys, where young individuals soon learn to avoid brightly marked insects.

Bearing the above in mind, it is no surprise that the Monarch has many mimics, such as the Viceroy (*Limenitis archippus*); there are others such as *Danaus (Salatura) genutia*, which are close relatives rather than mimics. Indeed, for many years it was called by the same scientific name as the Monarch, but is now recognized as being a different species altogether. There is, however, still disagreement as to the correct scientific name — whether it should be *Danaus genutia*, or *Salatura genutia*. The butterflies that are true mimics, such as the Viceroy, have evolved to look very similar to the Monarch in order to gain the advantage that birds will generally avoid them.

There is a similar, yet different form of imitation between species, called Mullerian mimicry. This differs from the Batesian form in that some chemically protected species have evolved to look very similar over many millions of years. This way, they all benefit from what is basically the same warning message, without potential predators having to learn that each individual species is distasteful.

Unfortunately for the Monarch, there are several birds that have evolved the ability to metabolize its toxins, so during the winter roosts, countless thousands are eaten by such species as the Black-Billed, Pallid

and Fan-tailed Cuckoos, the Cuckoo Shrike, and the Mockingbird. All is not lost, however, as the numbers in the bigger roosts can still deal with this sort of population predation. The smaller roosts are much more susceptible to any reduction in numbers, and this is one of the many reasons why several once-popular roost sites are disappearing. A single Mockingbird was observed once to virtually wipe out a small roosting colony.

The vivid colors of many species are, however, primarily for reproductive purposes. One of the problems when you're a butterfly is to work out which of the many other flying insects in your vicinity is of your species, and which of these is of the opposite sex. If you're a male, it may be very important to identify other males as soon as possible, so that you can chase them off before they steal any potential mates from you. To this end, each species has developed a unique signaling mechanism, of which color may only be a small part.

Many species beat their wings at a particular rate, and fly in a particular manner — this combined with the wing colors and patterns produces an overall visual message that will hopefully not get confused with those of other species. Some, however, do not just use visual signals, but back them up with chemical messages as well. The male detects the chemical, and homes in on it. The currently accepted explanation is that the male simply smells the female, and follows the scent trail. This is, however, an inadequate explanation for observed behavior, especially in some species of moths, where males can detect females at distances of several miles, against the wind.

It is possible that the chemicals produced, called pheromones, are being detected in some other manner. It is known that pheromones can produce very small electromagnetic signals when they react with oxygen, these being in the far infra-red region of the spectrum. It is also known that the spacing of the hairs on the male antennae are in the order of a quarter of one wavelength of the far infra-red, which is what they would have to be if they were going to work as some form of radio antenna. Is it therefore possible, that the males are homing in on a radio signal, rather than smell? It would certainly provide a more satisfactory explanation for observed behavior!

It's not just the females that produce scent, however. In many species, the males produce strong pheromones, with which they shower the females by fanning their wings whilst hovering near them. Some of the chemicals needed to produce these biological perfumes need to be acquired directly from certain plants by the males; often this is done by

Top: This Long-Tailed Blue has been attacked by something — probably a bird, which has taken a piece out of what it thought was the head, but was merely a set of false eye-spots!

Center: The *Danaus (Salatura) genutia* is one of the mimics of the Monarch and it is easy to see how the two can be confused, especially with the wings shut, as with this individual.

The European Peacock butterfly is particularly effective when it comes to flashing its eyespots at potential predators — especially while roosting during the winter. At this time, its wing muscles are cold, so immediate flight is impossible. It may be unnecessary to risk leaving its roost if it can scare away the intruder with a quick wing flash.

scraping the leaves or stems with their feet to make them ooze sap. This is then taken up via the proboscis, and processed for use later.

Another fascinating subject is that of how the colors are actually produced on a butterfly wing. Some species have evolved spectacular iridescent colors, such as the flashing sapphire blues of some of the Morpho family. These have become the focus of study for a research group at the Thin Film Photonics Group, in the School Of Physics, University of Exeter, where they are trying to discover just how these colors are produced. Their aim is to be able to reproduce this effect with industrial coatings — just imagine something like a car painted iridescent blue! See the section on current scientific work elsewhere in this book for more details of their project. Alternatively, you can access their web-site — the address is listed at the end of the book.

Butterfly colors are derived from thousands of scales on each wing. In fact, the Latin name for the butterfly family is "lepidoptera," which translates to "scale-wing." Each scale is arranged like the tiles on the roof of a house, the difference being that they are so small, that 250 of them laid end-to-end would only be an inch long!

If they are small in length, then this pales into insignificance when their thickness is examined — it would take over half a million of them laid on

top of one another to make a pile an inch thick! Each scale is intricately constructed to produce the iridescent effects that some species use so effectively. This is achieved because each scale is formed by a series of tiny layers of cuticle, sandwiched around layers of air.

The scales from different species are constructed in many different ways; some of them look like Christmas trees when they are sliced in half, and looked at end-on. It is the thickness of the layers, and the space of the air gap that separates them that determines the color that is produced. This is because only some of the light is reflected from the top surface, the rest travels through the thin film, until it reaches the lower surface, where it is reflected back through the film, until it exits from the top surface, and rejoins the light already reflected. At this stage, the two may be in-phase, or out of phase.

The extent to which this happens depends on the thickness and refractive index of the film, the angle at which the light strikes the film surface, and also the color of the light. If for a particular color the two reflected rays are in phase with each other when they rejoin, then they will combine to produce a bright reflection. If they are out of phase, they will cancel each other out, and that color will appear non-reflective. A really strong color is created by stacking the films on top of each other, with air gaps in between.

There is another form of deception practiced by butterflies, and that is to pretend to be an animal that you're not, or that your vulnerable head is actually somewhere far less vital, such as at the end of your wings. This is usually done by the use of some markings such as false eye-spots, although some butterflies use long "tails" to distract potential predators. These so-called tails, are in fact just extensions of the hind wings, shaped to fool chasing predators. They are usually structured to imitate antennae, especially amongst the Lycaenidae (the blues and hairstreaks). These butterflies have a habit of settling, and then slowly rubbing their hind-wings together. This slight motion causes the mock-antennae to twitch, just like the real thing, which no doubt confuses predators into thinking that the head is at the wrong end! In some species there are sideways projecting structures that give the false head a three-dimensional aspect; these can be most convincing even to the experienced eye.

Several butterflies use the contrast of dull camouflaged underwings, against the striking colors and markings of eye-spots above. When they settle, they sit with their wings closed, and if disturbed, they flash their wings open and shut, giving the impression that they are, in fact, a particularly fierce creature that should not be harassed further. An excellent example of this is the Peacock butterfly, *Inachis io*.

This Indian Leaf butterfly (*Kallima paralekta*) epitomizes the way some are able to mimic dead leaves. If this one had settled amongst those in the litter of a typical forest, it would be nigh on invisible to all but the closest inspection.

Conservation

The issue of butterfly conservation is guaranteed to provoke a passionate reaction from most nature lovers, although surprisingly, they can be very varied. There are two main camps; the first of which is generally "don't collect, don't own a net, don't even think about catching a butterfly, no how, no way." The second is typically "no collecting means no knowledge, which means no ability to monitor species biology, distribution, or population fluctuations." Those in the first group justify their attitude as being in the interests of conservation; ironically, so does the second group!

These are the two extremes, within which most of us fall. I personally don't collect at all (although I make up for this by collecting the books instead!), but I do sympathize with the scientific view that the current wave of extreme political correctness has lost the true perspective — the real threat to butterflies is not the occasional specimen taken by a collector, but is instead the major loss of habitat occurring all over the world.

In the old days, it was fashionable to own large cabinets with rows of butterflies of the same type — these are known as "series." The idea was to show a variation in size, shape and/or color. There is no justification in doing this anymore, unless it's for direct scientific purposes, such as a reference collection. If a new sub-species is found, how can you tell what it is without something to refer it to?

There is also the point that in well studied areas, there is little need to take specimens of butterflies, as most of them can be identified from a distance of several feet. This is not the case, however, with tens of thousands of species of moths, many of which need to be dissected under a microscope for correct identification. Take a look through any of the more scientific books on the subject, and you will be faced with endless, dull, detailed drawings of the genitalia of the various species. To give an example, let me quote from F. N. Pierce's book *The Genitalia Of The British Noctuidae*, published in 1909, concerning the identification of *Apamea furva*:

> "Furva: Harpe trigonate, indented at the crown, with corona; cucullus hairy; clasper strong pointed; ampulla slender; clavus produced, plain and rounded; uncus diamond shaped tip."

This is the identification list for a moth which I chose at random from some 70 pages of such descriptions. When I looked up the Latin name,

It is man's effect on the environment — typified by logging operations — that is the biggest threat to the world's butterfly population, not natural predators or the occasional collector.

The multiple issues of deforestation, pollution and global climate change are by far the biggest threats to successful butterfly conservation; sadly these are all caused by humankind.

the common name turned out to be the "Confused." Quite frankly, I'm not surprised!

I agree though, that collecting for collecting's sake should be discouraged, however, we have the real problem that we need to encourage young butterfly enthusiasts to take up the subject somehow. In the days of the great W. J. Holland, collecting was encouraged, as is evinced by this passage from his writing in *The Butterfly Book*, published in 1899:

> "There is no reason why every school of importance should not, in the lapse of time, secure large and accurately named collections . . . of the region in which it is located. Every high school should have a room set apart for the use of those students who are interested in the study of natural history, and they ought to be encouraged to bring together collections which should be properly arranged and preserved. The expense is not great, and the practical value of the training which such studies impart to the minds of young people is inestimable."

Without new generations of lepidopterists the future for butterfly conservation is bleak, so it is vital that we find some method of encouraging

youngsters to take up an in-depth interest in the subject. Maybe the answer is to foster a love of butterflies by getting kids to "collect" using photographic means, although I think it may be asking a bit much for kids to be able to afford such luxuries as film and its processing. Certainly when I was a child there was no way that I could have afforded a camera strap, let alone a camera!

There are many conservation projects going on all over the world, every one of which has to be centered on habitat management of some sort. Near where I live, a deal was struck with the local power company to take over management of the land underneath some of their high-voltage power cables, where they run along a fire-break through some woodland. This land is invaluable for butterflies, as there are few threats to their habitat, other than the uncontroled growth of unproductive tree species. There is no pesticide use, for instance, which makes a major difference to the viability of the local ecology. A group of volunteers, myself included, went into this area, and cleared it of unwanted scrub, and tried to encourage particular plants to grow, with the intent of providing the right habitat conditions for threatened butterfly species. Now, nearly 20 years later, it has blossomed into a major success. It is direct action like this that is needed everywhere.

As will be discussed later, the major causes of deforestation throughout tropical and temperate forests are commercial, such as logging and mining, but there are also other factors which include agricultural "reclamation," and the sacrificing of vast areas of land via flooding for the construction of reservoirs. One of the most insidious threats to all forms of plants and animals is chemical poisoning via widespread pollution and the use of pesticides.

The multiple issues of deforestation, pollution and global climate change are by far the biggest threats to successful butterfly conservation; sadly these are all caused by humankind. There is really only one avenue to travel down if we wish to make amends for the destruction that we have caused, and that is to influence matters at the governmental level. Most of the tropical forests of the world are in third-world countries that rely on financial aid from the first-world, so we can use this leverage to have real influence over the implementation of their conservation methods. At the end of the day most politicians are only concerned with two things — making money and getting re-elected. The real problem for us therefore is to know who to believe when we're voting!

Your own butterfly garden

One of the most popular ways of assisting with butterfly conservation is by planting lots of suitable food-plants in the garden. The most "help-ful" plants are those which flower late in the season — these can make a real difference to those butterflies which roost or hibernate, as they need to build up their fat reserves for the long winter ahead. The flowers need to be rich in nectar, and also attractive to butterflies in the first place. Good examples include the Valerian (*Valerianaceae spp.*).

One of the most popular ways of assisting with butterfly conservation is by planting lots of suitable foodplants in the garden. The most "helpful" plants are those which flower late in the season — these can make a real difference to those butterflies which roost or hibernate, as they need to build up their fat reserves for the long winter ahead. The flowers need to be rich in nectar, and also attractive to butterflies in the first place. Good examples include the Iceplant (*Sedum spectabile*), Valerian (*Valerianaceae spp.*), and the Michelmas Daisy (*Aster novi-belgii*). It is not so important to have plants that flower during the summer, as there are usually plenty around for the butterflies to choose from. However, if like most people you want to encourage butterflies whenever possible, it's a good idea to plant a wide range of flower species to maintain a food supply at all times. Those that flower early in the year will help the winter's survivors in early spring.

Some people also plant things which will be suitable for larval foodplants as well as for the adult butterflies. Nettles are very good for many of the "Nymphalids," so it is common for many well-meaning gardeners to leave a patch somewhere out of sight. Unfortunately, this is only too often behind a shed, or under some over-hanging trees where they won't get in the way. They then feel justified to say that they have "done their bit" in the cause of conservation; sadly though, the patch is usually damp and lacks sunlight. This will nearly always be rejected by discerning female butterflies, as they will not lay eggs where they are likely to fall victim to fungal problems caused by lack of warmth, ventilation and light.

How to keep and rear butterflies

Butterflies can be easy to raise from egg to adult, or they can be next to impossible, depending on the species. It also depends on how much time and money you are willing to expend, as you may have to provide specific conditions to rear them successfully. For instance, if you live in a cold area you may have to find a way to keep the temperature high enough for them to survive. Keeping them healthy through their various stages of development can be very demanding, and as mentioned earlier in the book, most species require their cages to be kept scrupulously clean, as they can be very susceptible to bacterial, viral or fungal infections.

One of the great advantages of rearing butterflies yourself is that it is almost certainly the easiest way to photograph them close up, particularly for species that are not local to your area. It is also by far the best way to record the entire life cycle, especially on film. The vast majority of the world's tropical species are known only by their adult form — we have no idea what their larvae look like or feed on. Any work that improves our knowledge in this direction is invaluable to science, and is one of the main areas where the amateur can really contribute new information.

One of the easiest ways to obtain livestock is to purchase from a dealer, or to swap them with another enthusiast. If you need to send them through the post, it's best done when they are still eggs. One of the problems though, is that by the time they arrive, any attached foliage will have wilted, and you must be careful that they are ventilated well enough to prevent any fungal growths. Once the eggs have hatched, you will have to decide how to feed the new larvae.

Once you have decided whether to use cuttings or potted plants, you will need a cage to put them in. You can either buy these, or make them yourself quite easily. If you do choose to build your own, it's a good idea to have a look at a few before you start construction — this may save you difficulty later on. The most important thing to remember is that condensation must be avoided at all costs, as it will encourage the dreaded fungal problems.

It's best, therefore, to use a fine netting for the sides of the cage, as this will allow light and fresh air in, and hopefully keep parasites and predators out. You need to bear in mind how the species you are keeping will pupate — and ensure that they have the right materials to achieve it. For instance, if they bury themselves in soft soil, you'll need to give them some peat or leaf mold. Don't just dig up some soil, as it could be harboring all sorts of nasties — mites, parasitic worms, and so on. Either sterilize it yourself or buy some that is sterilized. A do-it-yourself method is to stick it in the oven for a while. Bear in mind that it might stink when

If you are going to keep larvae, you will need a cage of some description. You can either buy them, or make them yourself quite easily. If you choose to build your own cage, it's a good idea to have a look at a few before you start construction — this may save you trouble later on. It's best to use a fine netting for the sides, as this will allow light and fresh air in, and — it is hoped — keep the parasites and predators out.

By far the best way to rear butterflies from the egg or caterpillar is to use potted plants instead of cuttings. This is the passion flower, larval foodplant of many butterfly species, including the Heliconids, such as the Zebra butterfly (*Heliconius charitonius*).

it gets hot — this could result in some interesting flavors for subsequent meals!

It is vital to check through any cuttings carefully before you place them in any cages, as it is only too easy to introduce insects or spiders that will be very happy to eat your precious larvae before you are even aware of their existence. Sometimes though, you can be pleasantly surprised — when I was a child, I once collected some fresh foodplant for some beloved hawkmoth larvae, only to find that I had unwittingly collected material that had more of the larvae already on it!

Another problem is that, when you throw out the old cuttings, you have to be careful not to throw out the larvae as well. As cuttings wilt, the leaves often curl up, resulting in nice convenient hiding places for shy larvae. You will also have to take care when the larvae are preparing to molt, as they must not be disturbed, or they may die.

The best way to provide foodplants is to have them planted in pots:, this way the larvae cannot crawl into the water jars. Having your food-plants — "potted up" may not be as simple as it sounds, as some species will strip a plant in no time, while others are cannibalistic, and so have to be kept apart. This means that you may need many plants ready, which can demand several months of planning, especially if the only way to obtain them is to grow them from seed.

Once you have raised your larvae, and they have gone through pupation and emerged successfully as adults, you will need to have nectar-providing plants for the butterflies to feed from. Good examples of that grow well in pots are the various species of buddleia, hebe, and sedums. The best way of all to choose what flowers to provide though, is undoubtedly to observe the butterfly species in the wild, and find out for yourself what they like to feed on.

Alternatively, you can feed them from solutions of honey or sugar and water, but it is very important that the strength of the solution is carefully controled. If the concentration gets too high, the sugars may re-crystallize in the butterfly's abdomen, giving it a slow and presumably painful death. The solution should be kept to around 5% honey. You can use artificial flowers to lead the butterflies to the honey solution, by inserting them into the neck of the container, or you can manually encourage the butterflies to feed by uncoiling the proboscis with a pin, and placing it on a pad of cotton wool soaked in a honey solution. If you have suitable flowering plants, it is probably easier to let the butterflies feed themselves, especially if you are new to rearing them!

If you decide to use sugar or honey solutions, bear in mind that these will act as attractants to wasps and ants, which will be a real threat to your butterflies. Another complication with rearing your own butterflies is that there are many other insects that will happily make a meal out of your prized "pets." The worst of these are the many parasitic flies and wasps, as most of them can detect and track down larvae, even when kept inside a house. Some of them are very small, so fine netting has to be used to keep them away. Spiders are also obviously likely to take any opportunity to get at your captives and feed off them.

If you are intending to breed the adults once they have emerged into nice healthy butterflies, you may have further problems. Some species will mate at the earliest opportunity (especially some moths, where the males will travel for miles to reach a female), but others require very particular light, temperature, and weather conditions, along with a lot of space, so that they can perform their highly complicated courtship flights. If you are lucky, you may be able to encourage them to pair by hand — this is where you hold the male in one hand, and the female in the other, and by encouraging the male to open his claspers and lock onto the female's abdomen, a pairing can sometimes be achieved.

It is also important that you keep the humidity level high, or else the butterflies will dehydrate and die. The easiest way to do this is to use a houseplant sprayer set to a fine mist. Use it several times a day to keep the air moist in the cages. You cannot use open trays of water, as the adults will drown in them, although you can use one if you cover it with netting. This will then slowly evaporate, helping maintain cage humidity.

Above: When attempting to get butterflies to pair, it is important to select individuals that are of the right age — if the male is too young he will not mate successfully, and if the female is too old, she will produce infertile eggs.

Below Left: Many butterflies will feed successfully from bowls of rotting fruit, soaking up juices from the fermenting bananas, apples, or whatever. The species that do well like this are a welcome change from those that require hand-feeding techniques!

Far Left: One of the great advantages of rearing butterflies yourself is that it is almost certainly the easiest way to photograph them close up, particularly for species that are not local to your area. This Giant Swallowtail (Papilio cresphontes) has just emerged from its pupal case onto a metal frame specially constructed for the purpose of obtaining clear pictures.

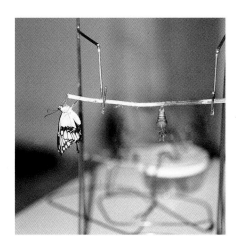

Identification tips

If you are new to identifying butterflies, it can seem a daunting task, especially if you're somewhere where there are a lot of similar species, such as fritillaries, blues or skippers. If you think this is hard though, try identifying some of the smaller moths! Seriously though, until you are very experienced, you will need the advice of others to reach a correct decision as to what you have been observing. The most obvious source of information is from books. At the end of this one, you will find an extensive bibliography to guide you in this direction. However, you could have all the butterfly books in the world, but without an experienced field worker for guidance, you would lose out on most of the "hands-on" knowledge that only accumulates with years of study.

If you don't have a local "guru" to approach for identification advice, the most important facility is the aforementioned set of photographs, or reference collection from which to make comparisons. There is, however, a new resource that is getting a lot of hype in the media, that can be used as a very useful identification tool, and that is the Internet.

Here's a good example of two similar species, the Pearly Heath (Right) and the Small Heath (Far Right). It may not look too hard to tell them apart here, but that is one of the reasons why photography is such an excellent aid to identification — if you were to try to get close enough to make out this level of detail with some species, you'd need an inordinate amount of luck and patience. Things get even harder when the two species in question are uncommon, so that it becomes almost impossible to make a back-to-back comparison without either a very good photograph or a reference collection to work from.

These pictures of the Small Pearl Bordered Fritillary (Above and Opposite page) and Pearl Bordered Fritillary (Center and Above Right) show just how difficult it can be to distinguish between two similar species. They make life even more difficult for the novice because their flight times overlap, and they fly in similar places. If, however, you're fortunate enough to get good photographs of them, their undersides can make things much easier, as can be seen from the pictures above. On the wing though, they can be very difficult to separate.

With computer technology racing ahead at full speed, many people have chosen to construct their own web-sites to show off their prowess with photographing or working with butterflies. This allows others to benefit from the hard work they have put in, and encourages a flow of knowledge between people working a long way apart — perhaps even continents away. If you have a picture of an unidentified specimen, it is far easier, cheaper, and faster to post it on your web-site, and have several experts pass back their opinions, than it is to have to take copies of it and send them all over the place! For some excellent examples of butterfly related web-sites, see the list of web addresses at the end of the book.

Once you are happy that an accurate identification has been achieved, you can then use your picture to help others build up their knowledge on the subject. It is possible that one day all the known species of the world will be posted within one web-site — what a superb reference library this would be! If different people or organisations were to collaborate to construct a database — for instance, if each took on a different family or subfamily, it could be a realistic project that could be added to as more knowledge was gained. It could then become a global resource, from which it would be possible to make identifications, look up foodplant requirements, find out about parasite relationships, and so on. Perhaps this is one way that we can encourage youngsters to take up the subject of lepidoptery — they could start building up a "virtual collection" of computer images, rather than catching live ones and "banging nails through them"!

The Butterflies

Rain forest, sub-tropical, and tropical species

The definition of "rain forests" for the purposes of this book is those that are found only within the world's tropical regions — including Africa, Asia, northern Australia, America, and countless islands in between. They all feature very high rainfall, some exceeding 12 feet a year! This combined with high temperatures produces the high humidity levels required by the fauna and flora that live within them.

One of the difficulties involved in studying rain forest butterflies is that not only are many of the best jungles in very remote places, but most species live in the canopies, which may well be 200 feet or more above the ground. The real problem, though, is that many are being deforested before we even get a chance to find and classify the vast numbers of species within them — especially the smaller invertebrates. In other words, we are making thousands of animals extinct, before we even know they exist!

There are two main reasons why deforestation is taking place — the superb growing conditions have resulted in huge numbers of hardwood trees, which are very attractive to logging companies. They construct crude roads to gain access to the deep forest, and then proceed to strip out the most valuable timber. The second stage happens when desperate peasants use the abandoned roads to find fresh ground on which to farm. They use "slash and burn" techniques to reduce the jungle to a thin layer of fine ash and cinders. This residue fertilizes the soil for a year or so, and then they have to move on. The plants can never reclaim the land because heavy rainfall washes the topsoil into rivers, clogging them up, and killing aquatic life for miles downstream.

It's never too early too start learning about butterflies! Here Professor Derek Partridge is studying species of "Graphium" swallowtails near the Zaire River, in Zaire, Africa. His assistant is his daughter Mischa. The rain forests of the world contain the greatest diversity of species found anywhere. Their high temperatures and humidity provide the ideal conditions for rapid growth — of plants as well as animals. The total lack of a winter allows many species to breed continually, which means that more generations are produced per year than anywhere else. This has resulted in the animals of the tropics having a huge evolutionary advantage over those of colder regions, where every winter their life cycles grind to a halt. This, in turn, has produced many strange and wonderful animals and plants — including many thousands of butterflies and moths.

This impressive Swallowtail shows how a mix of green and black can still produce dramatic coloration. Its common names include the Emerald Swallowtail, the Banded Peacock, the Burmese Banded Peacock, and the Moss Peacock. As can be seen here, it is keen on visiting nectar-rich flowers.

Common name:	Emerald Swallowtail
Latin name:	*Papilio (Princeps) palinurus/daedalus*
Descriptor:	Fabricius, 1787
Family:	Papilionidae *Latreille, 1809*
Subfamily:	Papilioninae *Latreille, 1809*
Tribe:	Papilionini
Genus:	Papilio *Linnaeus*
Subgenus:	Princeps *Hubner*
Species-group:	Palinurus *Fabricius*
Size:	3-3.5in (75-90mm)
Range:	Burma to Borneo and the Philippines

This impressive Swallowtail ranges across from Burma, through Borneo, and down into the Philippines. The sexes are similar, and both frequent woodland areas, where it is often abundant. It is the subject of much discussion concerning its classification — some list it as *Papilio daedalus*, whereas others list it as a subspecies of *Papilio palinurus*, whereupon it gets called *Papilio palinurus daedalus*.

Common name:	Emperor
Latin name:	*Morpho peleides*
Descriptor:	Kollar
Family:	Nymphalidae *Swainson, 1827*
Genus:	Morpho *Fabricius*
Size:	3.75–4.75in (95-120mm)
Range:	South and Central America, West Indies

This striking butterfly is one of the commoner members of the Morpho tribe. Over its vast range there are many sub-species, which, unsurprisingly considering its spectacular appearance, are the study of several projects researching their genetic relationships.

It takes about two and a half months for an Emperor Morpho to reach adulthood from the egg, with the larvae feeding on many different members of the Leguminosae family in the process. The pupae are green, and are suspended from plant stems or leaves. Once they have emerged, they are surprisingly long-lived as adults, surviving for up to nine months on the wing.

The male butterflies are much "bluer" than the females, with their highly iridescent wings sparkling vividly whenever the sun catches them. They inhabit hilly and forested areas, flying quite close to the ground, often along paths and stream beds, where they seem to be particularly sensitive to the brightness of the sun — if a cloud reduces the light for even a short time, they dive into the bushes and settle until it returns to an acceptable level.

The Emperor is one of the most spectacular of all butterflies, but unless you are willing to travel, you'll have to visit a commercial butterfly house for the chance to enjoy the incredible sight of its wings flashing in the sunlight. In the wild its comparatively long life-span allows it to learn about its local topography, which it covers on regular routes. This has often been its downfall, as collectors captured this evasive species by observing its routes, and then lying in wait with net in hand. An alternative method was to set baits of rotting fruit, preferably with the addition of sugary liquids. The females are more retiring than the males, which makes them seem rarer than they are. They spend a lot of time among the undergrowth.

The Dragontails are very unusual butterflies, for in flight they resemble dragonflies, beating their wings in a fast fluttering manner — they have more or less transparent wings, which, coupled with their habit of hovering over flowers, makes them seem even more unlike butterflies. They don't even stop fluttering when settled on a flower. To continue the dragonfly theme, they cohabit with them as well, flying in similar locations, such as stream beds and river margins.

Common name:	Green Dragontail
Latin name:	*Lamproptera meges*
Descriptor:	Zinken-Sommer, 1831
Family:	Papilionidae *Latreille, 1809*
Subfamily:	Papilioninae *Latreille, 1809*
Tribe:	Leptocircini
Species-group:	Dolicaon *Cramer*
Genus:	Lamproptera *Gray*
Size:	1.38-2in (35-50mm)
Range:	Northeastern India, southern China, Vietnam, the Malay Archipelago, and the Philippines

These striking butterflies are quite different to other members of the Swallowtail family, to which they belong. They have an extensive range, occurring from the Philippines, right up through the Malay Archipelago to north-eastern India, southern China, and Vietnam. They can be found living in forested regions up to elevations of 5,000 feet or so; there are 10 subspecies distributed across this range. They are regarded as a vulnerable species throughout the Malaysian Peninsula, but are less threatened elsewhere.

Common name:	Green Spotted Triangle
Latin name:	*Graphium (Graphium) agamemnon*
Descriptor:	Linnaeus, 1758
Family:	Papilionidae *Latreille, 1809*
Subfamily:	Papilioninae *Latreille, 1809*
Tribe:	Leptocircini
Genus:	Graphium *Scopoli, 1777*
Subgenus:	Graphium *Scopoli*
Species-group:	Agamemnon *Linnaeus*
Size:	3.3-4in (85-100mm)
Range:	Southern and northern India, southern China, the Malay Archipelago, east to Papua New Guinea, northern Australia and the Solomon Islands

The impressive Green Spotted Triangle is also called the Tailed Jay, or the Tailed Green Jay. It is a common butterfly, with an extensive range. Unusually these days, it is not considered to be a threatened species.

The many species of Graphium butterflies are all in the Swallowtail family, known as Papilionidae. There are about 130 in all, which are mainly African and Asian. This one, the Green Spotted Triangle or Tailed Jay, occurs from northern India right through to Australia, and in Papua New Guinea it is farmed commercially. It is a common butterfly, and has about 20 subspecies, with the larvae of all of them feeding mostly on members of the Annonaceae.

Here, the Indian Leaf butterfly (*Kallima paralekta*) demonstrates that only its underside has cryptic coloration.

Common name:	Indian Leaf
Latin name:	*Kallima paralekta*
Descriptor:	Horsefield, 1858
Family:	Nymphalidae *Swainson, 1827*
Genus:	Kallima *Doubleday*
Size:	3.5-4.5in (90–115mm)
Range:	India through the Malaysian Peninsula to Java

The Indian Leaf butterfly ranges all the way from Taiwan to India and Pakistan, favoring forested areas that receive heavy annual rainfalls. As is the case with so many rain forest butterflies, it has a weakness for rotting fruit, and is also often attracted to tree sap. When pursued by a predator (or excited scientist!) it flies at great speed, and then stops dead, seeming to disappear amongst the leaf litter of the forest floor. It does this particularly well, because the upper wings catch the eye's focus, being brightly colored; once it shuts its wings and dives to the ground though, it is very hard for the eye to follow. This is made even more difficult for the pursuer, as once it has landed, it tilts its body with respect to the sun, so that its shadow is minimized. They are known to be just as efficient at fooling birds as lepidopterists, which is borne out by the fact that it's a highly successful species.

Common name:	Malay Lacewing
Latin name:	*Cethosia hypsea*
Descriptor:	Doubleday
Family:	Nymphalidae *Swainson, 1827*
Genus:	Cethosia *Fabricius*
Size:	1.6-1.8in (42-45mm)
Range:	Burma, Malaysia to Sundaland

The Malay Lacewing, like so many other butterflies that are "aposematic" (possesses warning colors), has larvae that feed on passion flower vines — from which they gain chemical defenses.

It should be no surprise that the Malay Lacewing comes from Malaysia! It is not restricted to this country, but extends through into Burma, and down to Sundaland. The term "Lacewing" is due to the lacy pattern on the undersides of the wings. The larval foodplant is the passion flower, which provides it with chemical defenses — the adults are known to exude an unpleasant odor when handled.

The butterfly pictured here is a female Mocker Swallowtail (*Papilio dardanus*) — only the males have the characteristic "swallowtails" throughout most of their range — the exceptions are in Ethiopia and Madagascar, where the females still have them.

Common name:	Mocker Swallowtail
Latin name:	*Papilio (Princeps) dardanus*
Descriptor:	Brown, 1776
Family:	Papilionidae *Latreille, 1809*
Subfamily:	Papilioninae *Latreille, 1809*
Tribe:	Papilionini
Genus:	Papilio *Linnaeus*
Subgenus:	Princeps *Hubner*
Species-group:	Phorcas *Cramer*
Size:	3.5-4in (90-105mm)
Range:	Africa from Ethiopia to the Cape

The Mocker Swallowtail is an African butterfly, ranging from Ethiopia down to the Cape Province of South Africa. It is well known for the many distinct forms of the female, which yet again are mimics of unpalatable species, such as the Plain Tiger (*Danaus chrysippus*). The female no longer has the characteristic "swallowtails" throughout most of its range — the exceptions are in Ethiopia and Madagascar, although the male has retained them everywhere. The two sexes also differ in habits, with the female being "shy and retiring," and the male being more overt, flying in open sunshine along the edges of woods and rivers, as well as along trails. The larval foodplants are all members of the *Rutaceae*.

Common name:	Postman
Latin name:	*Heliconius melpomene*
Descriptor:	Linnaeus
Family:	Nymphalidae *Swainson, 1827*
Subfamily:	Heliconiinae
Genus:	Heliconius *Kluk*
Size:	2.4-3.3in (62-84mm)
Range:	Central and tropical South America

The tangled genetics of the Heliconius genus means that *Heliconius melpomene* is very difficult to distinguish from forms of *Heliconius erato*, which is a close relation.

The Heliconius genus of butterflies belong to the subfamily Heliconiinae, which in turn falls within the family Nymphalidae. They are some of the most interesting butterflies to occur anywhere in the world, and are a source of inspiration to many scientists. However, their tangled genetics cause much frustration and confusion to others. There are so many different forms of this one — *Heliconius melpomene* — for instance, that it is very difficult to distinguish some of them from various forms of *Heliconius erato*, which is a close relation. The unusually high number of subspecies of *Heliconius erato*, for example has made it the focus of many experiments into cross-breeding.

One of the most unusual things about the Heliconius butterflies is that they've evolved the ability to synthesise pollen as well as nectar from

Continued on next page

The larval foodplants of the Heliconius butterflies are members of the passion flower family (*Passifloraceae*) as shown here.

flowers. This may seem trivial, but it is highly significant to them, as they extract proteins from the pollen, whereas nectar is little more than sugar. This adaptation allows them to live as active adults for much longer than is usual in the butterfly world — up to nine months in some cases.

One reason why Heliconius butterflies manage to live for so long is that they are highly unpalatable to birds — this is due to the larval food-plants, which are members of the passion flower family (*Passifloraceae*). They contain all sorts of highly toxic chemicals, which are retained through the pupal stage into adulthood. This has resulted in them becoming "aposematic" — which simply means they're highly colored to warn off predators. As is discussed elsewhere in this book, when one species develops warning colors, others in the same locality often copy their colors to gain some protection themselves. Nowhere is this mimicry taken further than with the Heliconius butterflies, which form all sorts of complex Batesian and Mullerian mimicry relationships with many other butterflies, and lots of day-flying moths (see the section on "Coloration" for more on this topic).

The eyes of Heliconids are thought to be the most highly developed in the butterfly world, and many studies have been conducted into this. One such investigation discovered that early in the morning, the vision of males is highly biased towards yellow, which is the predominant color of their foodplant. Once they have had a chance to feed, their vision switches to being more biased towards red — the distinguishing color of the females.

The females also put their excellent eyesight to good use — while they are seeking suitable plants on which to lay their eggs, they will look to see if there are other caterpillars already on the plant, or whether eggs have been laid by another butterfly. This is because the larvae are solitary, and are cannibalistic. The plants have taken advantage of this by growing "false eggs" to try to fool the female into thinking that eggs are already present, so that she will fly off to another plant instead. Some females, however, actually test the "egg" to see if it is a real one or not! While she is checking out the plant for eggs and caterpillars, she will also look out for predators, and if she is not happy with the security of the plant, she will go elsewhere.

Common name:	Scarce Bamboo Page
Latin name:	*Philaethria dido*
Descriptor:	Linnaeus
Family:	Nymphalidae *Swainson, 1827*
Genus:	Philaethria *Billberg*
Size:	3.3-3.5in (85-92mm)
Range:	Tropical South and Central America

The Scarce Bamboo Page is a butterfly of tropical South and Central America. As an adult, it lives mainly in the tree-canopies, where it is a lover of direct sunshine. The larvae, however, feed lower down, on passion flower vines. They have a habit of chewing away at the end of a leaf until only the central rib remains — they then hide at the end of it to avoid their main enemy — the multitudes of ants that teem in the tropics.

The Scarce Bamboo Page is one of thousands of butterflies that "puddle." This is where the adult settles on damp ground and soaks up mineral salts with its proboscis. The reason for this seems to be reproductive — only males do it, and it is thought that the salts extracted are used in the spermatophore.

This butterfly from South and Central America belongs to the Nymphalidae family — it has the typical wing outline of a member of this family — compare it to the Mourning Cloak (*Nymphalis antiopa*) for instance.

Common name:	None
Latin name:	*Baeotus baeotus*
Descriptor:	Doubleday & Hewitson
Family:	Nymphalidae *Swainson, 1827*
Genus:	Baeotus *Hemming*
Size:	3.3-3.5in (85-90mm)
Range:	South and Central America

This butterfly does not have a generally recognized common name. It occurs through South and Central America, in such places as Columbia, Ecuador, and the Amazon Basin. It has such a strange contrast between the upperside and the underside of its wings that it has been suggested that it uses this to confuse its predators.

Common name:	Chequered or Lime Swallowtail
Latin name:	*Papilio (Princeps) demoleus*
Descriptor:	Linnaeus, 1758
Family:	Papilionidae *Latreille, 1809*
Subfamily:	Papilioninae *Latreille, 1809*
Tribe:	Papilionini
Genus:	Papilio *Linnaeus*
Subgenus:	Princeps *Hubner*
Species-group:	Demoleus *Linnaeus*
Size:	3.1-4in (80-100mm)
Range:	Iran, India, Sri Lanka, southeast Asia, to New Guinea and northern Australia

The Chequered, Lime, or Lemon Swallowtail is extremely widespread, being common in most areas where it occurs. It's probably a migratory species, taking advantage of the wide distribution of its foodplants, which are members of the citrus and legume families.

The Chequered, Lime, or Lemon Swallowtail is extremely widespread, occurring right across the Indo Australian region, from northern Australia, through to south-east Asia, and across the continental areas as far as Iran. It is common in most of these areas, and is probably a migratory species, taking advantage of the wide distribution of its foodplants, which are members of the citrus and legume families.

The Gulf Fritillary, or Silver Spotted Flambeau is a member of the sub-family Heliconiinae, and as such is another toxin-protected species. This seems to instil it with a total disregard for its own safety — its predators have learned the hard way that it will make them very sick if they eat it!

Common name:	Gulf Fritillary, or Silver Spotted Flambeau
Latin name:	*Agraulis vanillae*
Descriptor:	Linnaeus
Family:	Nymphalidae *Swainson, 1827*
Subfamily:	Heliconiinae
Genus:	Agraulis *Boisduval & Leconte*
Size:	2.6-2.8in (65-70mm)
Range:	North America through tropical America to Argentina

The Gulf Fritillary, or Silver Spotted Flambeau, is a member of the sub-family Heliconiinae and, as such, is another toxin-protected species. This is again due to the larval foodplant being various species of passion flower. Like many of the other Heliconids, it is very widely distributed, occurring from North America right down through Central and South America, as far as Argentina. Also in keeping with the others, it seems to have a total disregard for its own safety — gently fluttering around wherever it pleases — as indeed it can, because its predators have learned the hard way that it will make them very sick if they eat it.

Common name:	Red Pierrot
Latin name:	*Talicada nyseus*
Descriptor:	Guerin-Meneville
Family:	Lycaenidae *Leach, 1815*
Subfamily:	Lycaeninae *Leach, 1815*
Genus:	Talicada *Guerin-Meneville*
Size:	1.2-1.4in (30-36mm)
Range:	Sri Lanka, southern India, northern Burma

As an adult, the Red Pierrot can be abundant, but it is very localized and, as is often the case with its family, it is highly gregarious. It is such a weak flier that it is almost certainly chemically defended. It avoids the direct sunshine, preferring the security of the undergrowth. It is diurnal and crepuscular — that is it flies in the day, and through into the late evening. When it finally settles, it does so in groups, although no one knows how they find each other in such low light; possibly it is some form of scent assembly, or maybe they make acoustic signals — this is documented in other members of its family (but not for the purpose of assembly). In *The Butterfly Fauna of Ceylon*, L. G. O. Woodhouse describes this species as being easy to breed on *Bryophyllum calycinum*, which is its main foodplant on the island (nowadays known as Sri Lanka).

The Red Pierrot occurs from Sri Lanka, up through southern India, and into northern Burma, ranging from sea level up to elevations of 8,000 feet. It is a member of the extensive family of blues and hairstreaks; one of the characteristics of this family is that the caterpillars often have quite bizarre life histories, such as living in ant nests. This species is no exception, with the larva feeding inside the leaves of various succulent plants in the Stonecrop family (**Crassulaceae**). When it is ready to pupate, it does so on the outside of the leaf.

Temperate zones

The temperate butterfly species of the world include those found in general lowland areas, from scrub through to woodland. In stark contrast to butterflies from the tropics, those from temperate areas need to be able to deal with the extremes of weather found throughout the year. This has resulted in many adaptations to the problem of dealing with the harshness of winter.

The European (or Essex) Skipper passes through the cold winter months as an egg, whereas other species, such as the Duke Of Burgundy Fritillary and the Green Hairstreak, over-winter as a pupa, emerging in early summer as fresh butterflies, ready to capitalize on the new season.

Many other species survive through the winter as larvae — such as the Viceroy, which spins up a small tent-like structure. Some alpine species, however, have to endure temperatures as low as -70°F! These species have evolved a form of natural anti-freeze to allow them to deal with such extremes. This prevents the water crystals that form within their bodies from causing too much damage, especially when they expand as they thaw out.

The Mourning Cloak or Camberwell Beauty passes the winter as an adult, hiding away until the arrival of spring. It must face several hazards during this long harsh period; some predators may recognize it as a butterfly — it's much easier to remain concealed if you're an egg, small larva, or a pupa, than an adult. It must also ensure that the location it chooses for hibernation will remain stable through the winter. If the temperature should rise too much, its metabolism will speed up, and it will have to seek nourishment — if it gets too low, it will die. Likewise, if the humidity drops too far, it will dry out and perish. Nevertheless, every year enough survive to keep the species going!

Temperate zones range from lowlands to high mountains where it can be particularly cold. Temperate butterfly species need, therefore, the ability to deal with extremes of temperature.

The Giant Swallowtail, or Orange Dog as it is called in some places, is the largest butterfly of Northern America. As can be seen here, it is a magnificent butterfly — however, it is much more spectacular when seen on the wing, wheeling and swooping amongst the trees and bushes of the citrus groves where its foodplants are most common.

Common name:	**Giant** Swallowtail
Latin name:	*Papilio (Heraclides) cresphontes*
Descriptor:	Cramer, 1777
Family:	Papilionidae *Latreille, 1809*
Subfamily:	Papilioninae *Latreille, 1809*
Tribe:	Papilionini
Genus:	Papilio *Linnaeus 1758*
Subgenus:	Heraclides *Hubner*
Species-group:	thoas *Linnaeus*
Size:	4-5.5in (100-138mm)
Range:	Canada (Ontario), through U.S. to Costa Rica

Unlike so many other swallowtails, the Giant Swallowtail, or "Orange Dog," as it is called in some places, is not threatened — indeed it sometimes becomes a pest on citrus, which is one of its larval foodplants. It occurs from southern Canada, throughout the United States (east of the Rockies), through the southern states into Mexico, and down as far as Costa Rica (and possibly Columbia).

Common name:	Pipe-Vine Swallowtail
Latin name:	*Battus philenor*
Descriptor:	Linnaeus, 1771
Family:	Papilionidae *Latreille, 1809*
Subfamily:	Papilioninae *Latreille, 1809*
Tribe:	Troidini
Genus:	Battus *Scopoli*
Species-group:	Philenor *Linnaeus*
Size:	3-4.5in (75-114mm)
Range:	Southeast Canada through U.S. to Costa Rica

The Pipe-Vine Swallowtail is reasonably common throughout its range, as shown by the fact that so many female Tiger Swallowtails mimic it. This also shows that its coloration is well known to its predators; the fact that it is so well defended chemically, and yet does not have brightly colored markings is unusual.

The Pipe-Vine Swallowtail is unsurprisingly named after its larval food-plant, which is a member of the *Aristolochiaceae*. These are toxic vines, from which the caterpillars derive the poisons that protect them right through to adulthood. As we have seen with so many other chemically defended butterflies, it too is mimicked by others, including two papilios — the Black Swallowtail (*Papilio polyxenes*), and the female of the Spicebush Swallowtail (*Papilio troilus*), as well as by others.

Its range is similar to that of the Giant Swallowtail, occurring from southeastern Canada, throughout the United States and down as far as Costa Rica.

Above: The female adult of the Spicebush Swallowtail is a mimic of the Pipe-Vine Swallowtail, gaining protection by pretending to be unpalatable, when in reality it is edible.

Right: The yellow phase of the Spicebush Swallowtail is very similar to the Tiger Swallowtail (*Papilio glaucus*) – indeed, the whole group of these yellow and black butterflies are known as the "Tigers."

Common name:	Spicebush Swallowtail
Latin name:	*Papilio (Pterorurus) troilus*
Descriptor:	Linnaeus, 1758
Family:	Papilionidae *Latreille, 1809*
Subfamily:	Papilioninae *Latreille, 1809*
Tribe:	Papilionini,
Genus:	Papilio *Linnaeus*
Species-group:	Troilus *Linnaeus*
Size:	4-5in (100-1.26mm)
Range:	Southern Canada, U.S.

The female adult of the Spicebush Swallowtail is a mimic of the Pipe-Vine Swallowtail, gaining protection by pretending to be unpalatable when in reality, it is not. This is because its larval foodplants don't contain the necessary toxins. These plants include the Spicebush (*Benzoin*), Sassafras, Sweet Bay (*Magnolia*) and Zanthoxylum. In common with many other species of butterfly and moth, when disturbed the caterpillar has a defensive posture that makes it look like a small snake. It does this by swelling its head, and flicking it from side to side in a reptilian manner.

In some areas it is known as the Spicebush Swallowtail, but in others as the Green-Clouded Swallowtail. No matter what its name is, it's generally common throughout most of its range.

The magnificent Tiger Swallowtail is common throughout most of Canada, the United States, and Mexico. Watching these butterflies cavorting on a sunny spring morning is one of the great privileges bestowed on us by nature.

Common name:	Tiger Swallowtail
Latin name:	*Papilio (Pterourus) glaucus*
Descriptor:	Linnaeus, 1758
Family:	Papilionidae *Latreille, 1809*
Subfamily:	Papilioninae *Latreille, 1809*
Tribe:	Papilionini
Genus:	Papilio *Linnaeus 1758*
Subgenus:	Pterourus *Hubner*
Species-group:	Glaucus *Linnaeus*
Size:	4-6in (100-165mm)
Range:	Alaska, Canada, through U.S., to Mexico

The Tiger Swallowtail is well-known to anyone interested in nature who lives within its range. This includes Alaska, Canada, most of the United States, and northern Mexico. In some areas, the female mimics the black Pipe-Vine Swallowtail; there are also three distinct subspecies. The eggs are very large for those of a butterfly, and when they hatch the caterpillars conceal themselves by mimicking bird droppings. Once they have grown bigger, they turn green with large eyespots. They feed on a variety of foodplants, such as members of the willows (*Salicaceae*) and many prunus species, including cherry and plum.

Common name:	Dingy Skipper
Latin name:	*Erynnis tages*
Descriptor:	Linnaeus, 1758
Family:	Hesperidae *Latreille, 1809*
Genus:	Erynnis *Schrank, 1801*
Size:	1.2in (30mm)
Range:	Europe, temperate Asia

The Dingy Skipper is unusual for a butterfly in that it has quite drab and dull markings, and also because when it roosts for the night, it closes its wings like a moth, usually on the top of a plant that matches its wing coloration

The Dingy Skipper is unusual for a butterfly in that it has quite drab and dull markings. There is nothing dull about the way it flies though, for it has a brisk pace, flying low to the ground, and constantly changing direction — it's probably a real challenge for predators to pursue. When it roosts for the night, it closes its wings like a moth, usually on the top of a plant that matches its wing coloration. It can be found on limestone hills in locations where the larval foodplant, Bird's Foot Trefoil (*Lotus corniculatus*) grows.

Above and Right: The delicate little Duke Of Burgundy Fritillary can be found in association with its larval foodplants — primrose and cowslip (Primula spp.). It is a localized species, although it has a wide distribution.

Common name:	Duke of Burgundy Fritillary
Latin name:	*Hamearis lucina*
Descriptor:	Linnaeus, 1758
Family:	Nemeobiidae
Genus:	Hamearis *Hubner, 1818*
Size:	1.2-1.25in (30-32mm)
Range:	South and central Europe, central Russia

The Duke Of Burgundy Fritillary is a delicate little butterfly, which flies quite slowly, but with a fast wing-beat. It frequently basks in the sunshine on grasses and other low plants that are found in its natural habitat, which is downland and hillsides where its larval foodplants grow. These are Primrose and Cowslip (*Primula spp.*). It has a single brood each year, over-wintering as a pupa.

If you go by the name, it's no surprise that the **Green Hairstreak** is green: but it is unusual in the butterfly world, and its coloration is being studied in the **Thin Film Photonics Group at the University of Exeter.**

Common name:	Green Hairstreak
Latin name:	*Callophrys rubi*
Descriptor:	Linnaeus, 1758
Family:	Lycaenidae *Leach, 1815*
Genus:	Callophrys *Billberg, 1820*
Size:	1.25in (32mm)
Range:	Europe, northern Africa, temperate Asia, to the Pacific

The Green Hairstreak has as its name would suggest, a green coloration. This is only on the undersides though — the wings are brown on the upperside. There are very few butterflies that take advantage of green as the predominant color — one would have thought that many more would do so, but it only goes to show that there are higher priorities for them than blending in with vegetation.

This butterfly may be found on heathland, scrub regions and the outskirts of woods. Its main larval foodplants are Gorse (*Ulex europaeus*), Broom (*Sarothamnus scoparius*), and Bird's Foot Trefoil (*Lotus corniculatus*).

Common name:	Green Veined White
Latin name:	*Pieris/Artogeia napi*
Descriptor:	Linnacus, 1758
Family:	Pieridae *Duponchel, 1832*
Subfamily:	Pierinae *Swainson, 1840*
Genus:	Artogeia *Verity, 1947*
Size:	1.4-1.8in (35-45mm)
Range:	North America, Europe, Asia, Japan

The Green Veined White can be seen in fields and pastures throughout its range, wherever the larval foodplants can be found. These are similar to those of the Orange Tip, being crucifers such as Garlic Mustard and Charlock. It normally has two broods per year, over-wintering as a pupa.

The **Green Veined White** is often called a **Cabbage White**, although it is not a pest at all. It has a wide distribution, ranging across Europe, Asia, Japan, and North America. The female adult of this butterfly is unusual in having a scent that is easily detected by the human nose — it smells of lemons!

Like many other members of the Satyridae family, the Large Heath will fly in quite dull weather conditions. It is a butterfly of rough ground and bogs, with the larvae feeding on various grasses.

Common name:	Large Heath
Latin name:	*Coenonympha tullia*
Descriptor:	Muller
Family:	Satyridae *Boisduval, 1835*
Subfamily:	Coenonymphinae *Tutt, 1896*
Genus:	Coenonympha *Hubner, 1818*
Size:	1.6in (40mm)
Range:	North America, Europe, and temperate Asia

The Large Heath (or Ringlet as it is known in parts of the United States) can be found on peat bogs and rough meadows at elevations of up to 2,000 feet. There are many forms, known as "clines," which are spread throughout its range. In common with many other members of the family Satyridae, it is generally brown, with gold-edged rings on the underside. The larva feeds on things like Cotton Grass (*Eriophorum*), over-wintering whilst it is still quite small.

Common name:	Orange Tip
Latin name:	*Anthocharis cardamines*
Descriptor:	Linnaeus, 1758
Family:	Pieridae *Duponchel, 1832*
Subfamily:	Anthocharinae *Tutt, 1896*
Genus:	Anthocharis, *Boisduval, 1835*
Size:	1.75in (45mm)
Range:	Europe, Asia, Japan

The underside of the Orange Tip has a delicate tracery of green markings — this is a male.

The Orange Tip is a butterfly of late spring — in Europe it is one of the first signs that summer is on the way. Its favoured habitats are hedges and the edges of woodlands. Where it occurs it is common, being an active flier, with the males constantly on the patrol for females. These lack the orange tips to their wings, but have a similar intricate green pattern on their undersides. The females are very industrious, searching out food-plants and depositing a single egg per plant. The larval foodplants are in the *Cruciferae*, such as Garlic Mustard, and Cuckoo Flower. The caterpillars are highly cannibalistic, possibly to minimize the risks of being found by parasites.

Above and Right: The aptly named Orange Tip is a distinctive species, plentiful in late spring and early summer. Only the male has the bright orange markings as can be seen from the photograph of the two together (Right).

Common name:	Scarce Swallowtail
Latin name:	*Iphiclides podalirius*
Descriptor:	Linnaeus, 1758
Family:	Papilionidae *Latreille, 1809*
Subfamily:	Papilioninae *Latreille, 1809*
Genus:	Iphiclides *Hubner, 1820*
Size:	2.5-3.4in (65-85mm)
Range:	North Africa, Europe, Asia, China

The Scarce Swallowtail is one of the most impressive butterflies to be seen in Europe, although it also occurs in North Africa, throughout Asia, and into China. It occurs in two broods, with the adults flying in late May/early June, and also in late August/early September. Their flight is fast and furious, enabling them to cover ground at an impressive rate. They prefer agricultural or lowland areas, up to elevations of 6,000 feet or so. They particularly favor habitats that feature fruit orchards, which provide one of their main sources of larval foodplants; these include Peach (*Prunus persica*), Almond (*Prunus dulcis*), and Cherry (*Prunus*), but they also feed on Blackthorn (*Prunus spinosa*), Hawthorn (*Crataegus*), and Oak (*Quercus*).

The Scarce Swallowtail prefers agricultural or lowland areas, up to elevations of 6,000 feet or so. They are distributed through Europe, North Africa, Asia, and into China. They particularly favor habitats that feature the trees that provide their larval foodplants, such as those found in fruit orchards.

Above: The Comma Skipper, or Silver Spotted Skipper has many sub-species, some of which were at one time or another thought to be distinct species in their own right.

Right: The adults are fond of visiting flowers, flying from plant to plant in short up and down bursts — a habit which gave the family its common name.

Common name:	Silver Spotted Skipper
Latin name:	*Hesperia comma*
Descriptor:	Linnaeus, 1758
Family:	Hesperidae *Latreille, 1809*
Subfamily:	Hesperiinae *Latreille, 1809*
Genus:	Hesperia *Fabricius, 1793*
Size:	1-1.25in (25-32mm)
Range:	Europe, Asia, North America

The Comma Skipper, or Silver Spotted Skipper as it is known in Europe, has caused taxonomists endless problems. There are many subspecies, some of which were at one time or another thought to be distinct species in their own right. In the United States, this group includes the Manitoba, Boreal, Yosemite, Oregon, and Colorado Skippers, as well as several others.

Their preferred habitat is hilly limestone ground, where their foodplants are found. These are fescue grasses, on which the solitary caterpillar feeds through spring and into summer. The adult is fond of visiting flowers, which it does in short bursts of frenzied flight. This is also a characteristic of most other Skippers — hence their name.

The Silver Studded Blue is a butterfly of heathland, where it has an association with ants, as do so many of the other members of the Lycaenidae family. It is distributed throughout Europe, across Asia, and into Japan.

Common name:	Silver Studded Blue
Latin name:	*Plebejus argus*
Descriptor:	Linnaeus, 1758
Family:	Lycaenidae *Leach, 1815*
Subfamily:	Polyommatinae *Swainson, 1827*
Tribe:	Polyommatini *Swainson, 1827*
Genus:	Plebejus *Kluk, 1802*
Size:	0.85-1.0in (22-26mm)
Range:	Europe, temperate Asia including Japan

The uppersides of the wings of the male Silver Studded Blue are a bright purplish-blue, while those of the females are brown. The caterpillars feed on plants in the *Leguminosae* and *Ericaceae* families, where they are attended by ants that defend them against predators — in return they are given sugary liquids that exude from glands on the caterpillar's backs.

Common name:	Small Copper
Latin name:	*Lycaena phlaeas*
Family:	Lycaenidae *Leach, 1815*
Subfamily:	Lycaeninae *Leach, 1815*
Genus:	Lycaena Fabricius, 1807
Size:	1-1.25in (25-32mm)
Range:	Eastern North America, northern and eastern Africa, Europe, Asia, Japan

The Small Copper butterfly occurs in many countries across the world. In Europe its scientific name is *Lycaena phlaeas*, and the American subspecies is *Lycaena phlaeas americana*. It has a great deal of "spirit" — often chasing off much larger butterflies, and sometimes appearing quite unafraid to chase off animals and birds as well.

Throughout the Small Copper's range, the larval foodplants consist of members of the dock family (*Rumex*). This includes many of the "sorrels," such as Common Sorrel (*Rumex acetosa*) and Sheep's Sorrel (*Rumex acetosella*). In some parts of its range it over-winters as a pupa, and in others as a larva.

The Arctic or Chequered Skipper is a very localised butterfly, favoring clearings in upland forests. It flies much more weakly than the other members of the skipper tribe — this, combined with its distinctive markings, make it one of the easier members of this extensive family to identify.

Common name:	Arctic or Chequered Skipper
Latin name:	*Carterocephalus palaemon*
Descriptor:	Pallas, 1771
Family:	Hesperidae *Latreille, 1809*
Subfamily:	Heteropterinae *Aurivillius, 1925*
Genus:	Carterocephalus *Lederer, 1852*
Size:	1.1in (28mm)
Range:	Europe, Asia, Japan, North America

In the United States, this butterfly is known as the Arctic Skipper, whereas in Europe it is referred to as the Chequered Skipper. It favors clearings in upland forests, where it flies much more weakly than the other members of the Skipper tribe. The caterpillar feeds on species of brome and other grasses, and then overwinters while fully grown. It pupates in the spring, and the adult emerges at the beginning of June.

Common name:	European or Essex Skipper
Latin name:	*Thymelicus lineola*
Descriptor:	Ochsenheimer, 1808
Family:	Hesperidae *Latreille, 1809*
Subfamily:	Hesperidae *Latreille, 1809*
Genus:	Thymelicus *Hubner, 1819*
Size:	0.95-1.1in (24-28mm)
Range:	Europe, Asia, North America

Most Skippers hold their wings in this unusual manner. There are many other features of this family that set them apart from other butterflies, causing the scientists all sorts of headaches as they try to sort out their taxonomic classification!

This is a European species, where it is known as the "Essex Skipper." It had its range extended artificially somewhere around 1910 when it was accidentally introduced to Ontario. It has since spread its range down into Michigan and Ohio, and in some places is so numerous that it has become a pest of grasslands.

It prefers open ground, meadows and hillsides, where the larvae feed on various grasses. There is one generation a year, over-wintering as an egg. Essex Skippers can be found anywhere from sea level to elevations of around 6,000 feet.

The Mourning Cloak or Camberwell Beauty ranges through North America, Europe, and Asia. In the early days of lepidoptery — the 18th and 19th centuries, this was considered one of the most prized of specimens to obtain. Many were caught on the European mainland, and fraudulently sold in Britain to gullible collectors as being native.

Common name:	Mourning Cloak or Camberwell Beauty
Latin name:	*Nymphalis antiopa*
Descriptor:	Linnaeus, 1758
Family:	Nymphalidae *Swainson, 1827*
Genus:	Nymphalis *Kluk, 1802*
Size:	2.4-2.5in (60-65mm)
Range:	North America, Europe, Asia

This spectacular butterfly is known in the United States as the Mourning Cloak, where it can be found almost everywhere. In Europe though, it is called the Camberwell Beauty; this derives from the first record in England, when it was seen at Cool Arbour Lane, near Camberwell, London, in 1748.

When the butterfly is settled with its wings closed, it is well camouflaged against tree trunks or branches. The larval foodplants are Willow (*Salix*), Elm (*Ulmus*), Poplar (*Populus*), and Hackberry (*Celtis*).

Common name:	Question Mark
Latin name:	*Polygonia interrogationis*
Family:	Nymphalidae *Swainson, 1827*
Genus:	Polygonia *Hubner, 1818*
Size:	2.4-2.6in (62-66mm)
Range:	Canada, U.S.

The Question Mark is common through southern Canada and the United States (east of the Rockies). As with its relation, the Comma, it is extremely well camouflaged when sitting with its wings shut — this is because the edges of the wings are jagged, giving them a silhouette just like a dead leaf. This impression is backed up even further with colors and markings that make this illusion look very convincing. The caterpillars feed on Elm (*Ulmus*), Hackberry (*Celtis*), and Nettle (*Urtica*), as well as many other plants.

The Question Mark is so named because on the undersides of it wings there is a silver line and a dot in the shape of a question mark. In Europe there is a very close relation which has the mark in the shape of a comma, so unsurprisingly, it is called the Comma!

Above: The White Admiral is a very localized species, having its distribution constrained by the very specific requirements of its larval foodplant — it needs small isolated "trails" of Honeysuckle (*Lonicera*)

Right: The underside is beautifully marked, although the most impressive feature of this butterfly is its flight pattern — swooping and gliding through leafy woodland glades on its hunt for flowers or a mate.

Common name:	White Admiral
Latin name:	*Ladoga camilla*
Descriptor:	Linnaeus, 1763
Family:	Nymphalidae *Swainson, 1827*
Subfamily:	Limenitininae *Butler, 1869*
Size:	2-2.4in (52-60mm)
Range:	Europe, temperate Asia including Japan

The White Admiral is a delight to watch as it "floats" through the woods it inhabits. It is a very localized species, with the larval foodplant dictating where it can survive. This is Honeysuckle (*Lonicera*), however, the female butterfly will reject all those except small isolated plants. No one knows why, but it is highly likely that this is to try and avoid either predation or parasitism, or perhaps even both.

The winter is passed as a half-grown larva, with the adult making an appearance at the beginning of July. Whilst on the wing, the adult will visit flowers for nectar, and also settle on damp ground to obtain mineral salts.

Mountain/alpine and hill species

The butterflies of mountainous regions have to be able to withstand severe extremes of weather throughout the year. The long winters of some areas mean that alpine butterflies may only have a few weeks in which to undergo the transition from egg to adulthood. This has a drastic effect on the number of species that are able to survive, resulting in them being very few and far between. This is in stark contrast to tropical rain forests where the numbers of species are staggering to comprehend, especially among the moths.

Those species which inhabit hilly areas generally have an easier time of it, but even so, there are far fewer species than in the lowlands. The basic criterion is the average temperature, so upland regions nearer the equator have a greater diversity than those towards the poles.

Right: This view of a craggy Pyrenees skyline shows the favored habitat of the Apollo butterfly. Terrains such as this are also ideal for species of Festoons and many of the Satyrs (Family Satyridae).

Far Right: Some mountainous regions are really productive for butterfly species, such as the Atlas mountains, pictured here. As you move north though (or to higher altitude), the environment gets increasingly harsh, and the number of species able to survive there decreases dramatically.

The Alaskan or Old World Swallowtail is one of the success stories of the family.

Common name:	Alaskan or Old World Swallowtail
Latin name:	*Papilio machaon*
Descriptor:	Linnaeus, 1758
Family:	Papilionidae *Latreille, 1809*
Subfamily:	Papilioninae *Latreille, 1809*
Tribe:	Papilionini
Genus:	Papilio *Linnaeus*
Subgenus:	Papilio *Linnaeus*
Species-group:	machaon *Linnaeus*
Size:	3-4in (75-100mm)
Range:	Europe, Asia, Japan, Alaska, northern Africa

This butterfly has many different common names; in the United States, it is known as the Alaskan or Old World Swallowtail, whereas in the United Kingdom it is known simply as the Swallowtail — but this is because it is the only one to occur there, so there's no risk of confusing it with others! As a species this is one of the success stories of the family, for it ranges right around the world in what is known as the "Palearctic Region." This includes Alaska, Russia, China, Japan, northern India, and Europe. It even occurs as far south as the mountains of Yemen, in the Middle East.

Common name:	Apollo
Latin name:	*Parnassius apollo*
Descriptor:	Linnaeus, 1758
Family:	Papilionidae *Latreille, 1809*
Subfamily:	Parnassiinae *Swainson, 1840*
Tribe:	Parnassiini
Genus:	Parnassius *Latreille*
Species-group:	apollo *Linnaeus*
Size:	2-4in (50-100mm)
Range:	Europe, central Asia, China

The Apollo butterfly is the first one to spring into the minds of most lepidopterists when mountainous regions are mentioned. It is protected by law in many countries, but this doesn't stop people continuing to take them for commercial profit.

The Apollo butterfly is a member of the subfamily Parnassiinae, as are both of the Festoons. When lepidopterists speak about mountainous regions, this is the species that most think of first. It is rare in western Europe although in parts of its massive range it is quite common. Its distribution covers most of sub-alpine Europe, central Asia and parts of China. It is protected by law in many countries, but even where this is so, some people continue to take them for trading purposes. It flies from May to September over the rocky slopes that form its habitat.

Above: The Eastern Festoon visits flowers frequently, often presenting the ideal opportunity to get close enough to obtain clear photographs.

Right: The Eastern Festoon is a typical butterfly of lower mountains, flying on ground up to about 4,000 feet above sea level. The caterpillars feed on various species of Pipe-Vines, from which they acquire their unpalatability to birds.

Common name:	Eastern Festoon
Latin name:	*Allancastria cerisyi*
Descriptor:	Godart, 1824
Family:	Papilionidae *Latreille, 1809*
Subfamily:	Parnassiinae *Swainson, 1840*
Tribe:	Zerynthiini
Genus:	Allancastria *Bryk*
Size:	1.5-2.25in (40-60mm)
Range:	Sotheast Europe, Turkey, the Middle East

The Eastern Festoon is a typical butterfly of hills and lower mountains, being localised and sometimes quite rare. In a few countries, such as Greece, it is protected by law. It will fly on ground up to about 4,000 feet above sea level. It is distributed throughout southeastern Europe, the Caucasus mountains of Russia, into Turkey and much of the Middle East. Like so many lowland species, its larval foodplants are various species of Pipe-Vines (*Aristolochiaceae*), which gives them some degree of unpalatability to birds.

The False Apollo is highly unusual in the butterfly world in that it has almost no coloration on its fore wings. This is, however, quite common amongst the moths, especially those which mimic bees, wasps and hornets. It is especially strange for this butterfly to have so few markings, as its larvae feed on Pipe-Vines, and so are chemically defended. Such species usually warn predators of such toxins with bright markings.

Common name:	False Apollo
Latin name:	Archon apollinus *Herbst, 1798*
Family:	Papilionidae *Latreille, 1809*
Subfamily:	Parnassiinae *Swainson, 1840*
Tribe:	Parnassiini
Genus:	Archon *Hubner*
Size:	1.5-2in (40-50mm)
Range:	Southeast Europe, Lebanon, Syria, Jordan, Israel, Armenia, Iraq, Iran

The False Apollo is a very strange looking butterfly, having almost no coloration on its fore-wings. It inhabits rocky and scrub regions up to 5,000 feet above sea level throughout its range; this covers south-eastern Europe, down through Lebanon, Syria, Jordan, Israel, and across into Armenia, Iraq and Iran. The adult emerges very early in the year, flying in March and April, when the females seeks out the larval foodplants, which, as with the others in this subfamily, are various species of Pipe-Vines (*Aristolochiaceae*).

Common name:	Southern Festoon
Latin name:	*Zerynthia polyxena*
Descriptor:	Denis & Schiffermuller, 1775
Family:	Papilionidae *Latreille, 1809*
Subfamily:	Parnassiinae *Swainson, 1840*
Tribe:	Zerynthiini
Genus:	Zerynthia *Ochsenheimer*
Size:	1.5-2.25in (40-60mm)
Range:	Southern Europe, western Turkey, southwestern Russia

The Southern Festoon, like many alpine species, will often take the opportunity to bask — rocks are particularly good locations for this because when they are hot they radiate heat, so the butterfly gets warmth from underneath as well as from above.

The Southern Festoon, or "Birthwort Butterfly" has a similar habitat to its close relation, the Eastern Festoon, being a butterfly of hilly and rocky regions, where it will fly at elevations of up to 3,000 feet. It also feeds on Pipe-Vines (*Aristolochiaceae*) when it is a caterpillar, so it too has chemical defences giving justification for its warning coloration. It has much the same distribution, but does, however, occur in southern France and Italy as well. It is not as rare as the Eastern Festoon through most of its range, though in Russia and much of Europe its status is considered to be "vulnerable."

The Blue Pansy or Blue Argus is a member of the Nymphalidae family, which with over 5,000 species, has more than any other such group of butterflies. In all parts of the world, in stark contrast to their seeming beauty, the multitudinous Nymphalids enjoy visiting and feeding off rotting fruit, decomposing animal remains, or other such delicacies!

Common name:	Blue Pansy
Latin name:	*Junonia orithya*
Descriptor:	Linnaeus
Family:	Nymphalidae *Swainson, 1827*
Genus:	Junonia *Hubner*
Size:	1.5-2.4in (40-60mm)
Range:	India, Africa, southern Asia, China, the Philippines, Indonesia, Papua New Guinea, Australia

The Blue Pansy is a common butterfly, with various subspecies throughout its wide range, which extends from the Afrotropical region, across Asia, into the Orient, and down to Australia. It will fly anywhere from sea level, up to about 9,000 feet, preferring open dry ground to more wooded areas. The larval foodplant is usually one of the various species of *Acanthaceae* or *Scrophulariaceae*.

Common name:	Long-Tailed Blue
Latin name:	*Lampides boeticus*
Descriptor:	Linnaeus 1767
Family:	Lycaenidae *Leach, 1815*
Subfamily:	Polyommatinae *Swainson, 1827*
Tribe:	Lampidini *Tutt, 1907*
Genus:	Lampides *Hubner, 1819*
Size:	1-1.4in (25-35mm)
Range:	Europe, Africa, Asia, Australia, Hawaii

The Long-Tailed Blue is a another migratory species, occurring across most of Europe, Africa, and Australia. It does not occur in the continental United States, although it has colonised Hawaii as a result of an accidental introduction somewhere around 1880. It is one of the most widely-distributed "blues," although it cannot over-winter in cold climates. This wide range is partly due to the fact that its caterpillars will feed off almost any of the legume family — these include peas and beans, which occur right across the world.

The false eye-spots and "mock antennae" on the hind wings are an excellent illustration of deceptive coloration and patterning — see the picture in the section on coloration for an actual example of one which was unsuccessfully attacked by a bird.

The **Long-Tailed Blue is typical of many members of the Lycaenidae family, in that the males are much more brightly colored than the females, as can be seen here, with the male pictured (Above) and the female (Below). It is a migratory species that has colonized most temperate regions, although the closest it has got to the United States mainland is Hawaii, where it was an accidental introduction somewhere around 1880.**

There are many butterfly species which have such large distributions that it is impossible to say that they belong in any one particular habitat. Most are successful, often because their foodplants are also widespread. Many of the butterflies which onlookers regard as "locals," such as the Red Admiral and the Monarch are in fact migrants that could have originated hundreds, if not thousands of miles away! In the spring, those individuals which have survived the winter begin moving northwards. One of the first things they must do before they can travel very far, is to find flowering plants from which they can gain nourishment to replenish their energy levels — flight is energetically expensive!

Common name:	Monarch
Latin name:	*Danaus plexippus*
Descriptor:	Linnaeus 1758
Family:	Danaidae *Bates, 1861*
Subfamily:	Danainae, *Boisduval*
Tribe:	Danaini, *Boisduval*
Genus:	Danaus *Kluk, 1802*
Size:	3-4in (75-100mm)
Range:	North, Central and South America, Australia, New Zealand, Southeast Asia, the Canary Isles

This butterfly is known as the Monarch in the United States, as the Monarch or Milkweed in Europe, and as the Wanderer in Australia. It is one of the widest-ranging butterflies in the world, with its migration and roosting habits becoming the focus of numerous television programs, radio broadcasts, books, and magazine articles. These have made it notorious, and it is a major tourist attraction at its over-wintering sites. These are spectacular, with many millions of individual Monarchs in the larger roosts.

In North America, the year starts with the adult Monarch leaving its winter roost site, and making its way north, seeking nourishment from flowering plants as it does so. By late summer, several broods will have occurred, and the descendants of the over-wintering adult may well have

reached Canada. They then turn south, and return to the winter roost sites of their ancestors. These are in a variety of locations, including Florida, New Mexico, Mexico and California.

As mentioned earlier in this book, the Monarch uses toxins acquired from the larval foodplants (*Asclepiadaceae*) to build up a chemical defence against potential predators. These poisons are known as "cardenolides," and are highly effective against many animals, including most birds. It is, however, defenseless against things like the Praying Mantis. There are many other animals that will eat Monarchs as well, such as lizards, mice, dragonflies, and some birds.

Above: Hanging about upside-down might seem a strange way to pass the day, but this female is laying eggs — a hazardous time, for all sorts of predators may be lurking amongst the foliage.

Below: Feeding can be just as hazardous . . .

The Plain Tiger is the species illustrated in the famous Ancient Egyptian tomb fresco known as "Fowling In The Marshes," where seven clearly recognisable individuals can be seen. This is the earliest recorded depiction of butterflies in human art.

The larval foodplants of the Plain Tiger are many and varied, but tend to be *Asclepiadaceae, Rosaceae, Euphorbiaceae, Scrophulariaceae, Plumbaginaceae,* or *Convolvulaceae.*

Common name:	Plain Tiger or African Monarch
Latin name:	*Danaus chrysippus*
Descriptor:	Linnaeus 1758
Family:	Danaidae *Bates, 1861*
Subfamily:	Danainae, *Boisduval*
Tribe:	Danaini, *Boisduval*
Genus:	Danaus *Kluk, 1802*
Size:	2.5-3.25in (65-80mm)
Range:	Canary Islands, Africa, Middle East, Japan and Southeast Asia to New Guinea, Australia, and Fiji

This butterfly is known variously as the Plain Tiger, African Monarch, Lesser Wanderer, or the Golden Daniid. It is almost as widespread as the Monarch, covering Africa, Asia, and Australia, but not North or South America. Like its relatives, it shares with the Monarch and the Queen in being unpalatable to birds, which is one of the reasons it is so successful as a species. Another factor is that in some tropical places it can produce up to 12 broods a year! This is reduced to one or two a year in colder climates. It is a slow flier, preferring open country to more forested areas, so it is one of the few species that is benefiting from the deforestation of most tropical countries. It does not have to be a fast flier as it is another that is usually chemically defended as a result of its larval foodplants.

Common name:	Queen
Latin name:	*Danaus gilippus*
Descriptor:	Cramer
Family:	Danaidae *Bates, 1861*
Subfamily:	Danainae, *Boisduval*
Tribe:	Danaini, *Boisduval*
Genus:	Danaus *Kluk, 1802*
Size:	2.75-3in (70-75mm)
Range:	Southern U.S., Central America, including Mexico

The Queen is another member of the Milkweed family, the Danaidae, along with the Monarch. Its larvae also feed mainly on Asclepiadaceae, though not exclusively. Those that do are highly distasteful to most predators, especially birds. Unlike its relative though, it is not migratory. It ranges across the southern United States, through Mexico and into Central America. It is commonest in the Gulf States, where it outnumbers the Monarch, as a result of which several other butterfly species have mimicked its coloration.

The Queen is a relative of the Monarch, and (for those whose caterpillars fed on Milkweed) also has chemical defenses acquired from the larval stage. Although it is not a close relation, in Trinidad there are subspecies of both the Queen and the Monarch that look very similar — it is thought this is because most Queen butterfly caterpillars there do not feed on plants containing toxins. By evolving similar markings and coloration to the Monarch, they have gained a degree of protection from predators.

As soon as the season's fruit ripens, the Red Admirals will take advantage of any early fallers, feeding off the juices which ooze freely as the tasty remains decompose.

Common name:	Red Admiral
Latin name:	*Vanessa atalanta*
Descriptor:	Linnaeus 1758
Family:	Nymphalidae *Swainson, 1827*
Subfamily:	Nymphalinae *Swainson, 1827*
Genus:	Vanessa Fabricius 1807
Size:	1.75-2.25in (45-60mm)
Range:	North America, northern Africa, Europe, Asia Minor

The Red Admiral is really a species of milder climates. It does hibernate, though it rarely, if ever, survives the winter in regions where there is any serious freezing. Every year it migrates northward from late spring onwards, until the temperatures drop at the end of summer, when it seems to start a return migration southwards. At this time, it is often to be found on rotting fruit, when it sometimes gets inebriated by the natural alcohols produced by the fermenting fruit juices. When it gets to this state, it can be easily picked up by hand, whereupon it will happily sit in a drunken stupor!

Its distribution is extensive, in the New World it ranges from Canada to Central America, and in the Old World, from North Africa, right through Europe and Asia Minor to Iran. The larval foodplant is usually nettles, but it will also feed on hops.

Common name:	Small White or Cabbage White
Latin name:	*Pieris/Artogeia rapae*
Descriptor:	Linnaeus 1758
Family:	Pieridae *Duponchel, 1832*
Subfamily:	Pierinae *Swainson, 1840*
Genus:	Artogeia *Verity, 1947*
Size:	1.75-2in (45-55mm)
Range:	North Africa, Europe, Asia, Japan, North America, Australia

The Small or Cabbage White is a highly migratory species

This butterfly's common name is the Small White, although it is known throughout the world as the Cabbage White. It is a major pest of cabbages, lettuce, and nasturtiums (*Brassicaceae* and *Tropaeolaceae*) across the world, for it occurs in Europe, North Africa, Asia, Japan, Australia and North America. It only reached the American continent by the hand of mankind, when it was accidentally introduced into Quebec in 1860.

It is a highly migratory species, sometimes crossing land and sea in large numbers. It will survive in most habitats up to heights of about 6,000 feet.

Reference

Web sites

I have chosen just a few of the thousands of web-sites available. The first few are from Britain, the rest are just a selection of the many that I found in a couple of hours of web-surfing. If you are new to the internet, just type in "butterflies" as your search string, and you will find more than you can cope with! All those below were functional at the time of writing, and all are well worth a visit, with some superb information and images displayed. I don't know how long the "site-masters" intend to keep these sites running — for the sake of those reading this book, I hope they do so for some time to come!

The Alaskan or Old World Swallowtail is one of the success stories of the family .

http://eng10.ex.ac.uk/~pbhook
This is my site! Here you can see what else I've been up to: other books and research projects — and the various other ways I keep myself amused.

http://newton.ex.ac.uk/research/thinfilms/
This is home to research into butterfly wing coloration at:
Thin Film Photonics, Department Of Physics, University Of Exeter, England.

http://eng10.ex.ac.uk/group/chris/
This is home to the Materials Research Group, at the School Of Engineering and Computer Science, University Of Exeter, England.

http://www.captain.ndirect.co.uk
Captain's European Butterfly guide — at the time of writing, this featured 99 mostly European species. Simon Coombes, or "Captain" is a wildlife photographer. His superb photographs have been used extensively throughout this book.

http://butterflywebsite.com/gallery/index.htm
A huge number of excellent galleries of butterfly sites

http://www.fortnet.org/~paulevi/index.htm
This is Paul Opler's site, he is an experienced author and photographer.

http://users.sedona.net/~wah/
This site features butterflies of Sedona.

http://www.hultsfred.se/users/t/tgorw/paindex.htm
This site is devoted to the Parnassius butterflies of the world.

http://www.aa6g.org/Butterflies/tropical.html
This site is devoted to tropical butterflies, including many beautiful bird-wings, (Ornithoptera), morphos (Morphidae), and swallowtails (Papilionidae).

http://www.mgfx.com/Butterfly/society/cba/chcklist.htm
This site is a checklist of the Butterflies of Connecticut, with photographs by Jeff Young.

http://www.chebucto.ns.ca/Environment/NHR/lepidoptera.html
This site calls itself the "Electronic Resources on Lepidoptera," and entitles itself "the most complete and comprehensive web-site on lepidoptera on the Internet!" It offers both information about butterflies and moths as well as "a comprehensive set of pointers to other sources of electronic information on lepidoptera."

Bibliography

Over the years, many thousands of books have been written about butterflies and moths. My personal favorites are those written before 1900; this is for several reasons, firstly many were exquisitely illustrated, with hand-colored plates that could only have been commercially viable back then. They were printed in outline, and day after day, teams of old ladies would color them in by hand! Another reason that they appeal to me is that before this date, the authors weren't afraid to write what they saw and felt, and do so in a lively and interesting manner — this gave a feel for their (often eccentric) personalities.

After about 1900, many authors seemed to feel the need to try and adopt a more "scientific" style, which filtered out a lot of their atmosphere — I think this is a sad loss, as to me they become dry and uninteresting without anecdotal content. There are, however, many excellent books written since then — unfortunately far too many too list here.

The books listed below vary from those suitable for novices who just want some guidance, through to titles more suited to serious academics. Where they exist, I have included the ISBN reference, which will help you access them. Some of the titles were out of print a hundred years ago, so if you want to purchase these, you'll have to hunt for them — a good winter-time activity when the natural world is slumbering through the cold!

Two-Tailed Pasha (*Charaxes jasius*).

Ackery, P. R. and Vane-Wright; R. I.; *Milkweed Butterflies — Their Cladistics & Biology*; Cornell, 1984 (ISBN 0-8014-1688-4).

Baines, V. and Dunbar, D.; *Glorious Butterflies and their flora*; Butterfly Conservation, 1993 (ISBN 0-9512452-8-7).

Barcant, M.; *Butterflies of Trinidad and Tobago*; Collins, 1970 (ISBN 0 00 212027 5).

Barrett, C. and Burns, A. N.; *Butterflies of Australia and New Guinea*; 1951.

Barrett, C. G. *The Lepidoptera of the British Islands* vol. I; Reeve & Co, 1893.

Black, D.; *Carl Linnaeus — Travels*; Paul Elek, 1979 (ISBN 0-236-40177-7).

Emmel, T. C.; *Butterflies*; Thames & Hudson, 1976.

Bristow, C. R., Mitchell, S. H. & Bolton, D. E.; *Devon Butterflies*; Devon Books, 1993 (ISBN 0-86114-884-3).

Brooks, M. & Knight, C.; *A Complete Guide to the British Butterflies*; 1982 (ISBN 0-224-01958-9).

Brown, F. M. & Heineman, B.; *Jamaica and Its Butterflies*; 1972 (ISBN 0-900848-448).

Chatfield, J.; *F. W. Frohawk, His Life and Work*; 1987 (ISBN 0-946284-68-7).

Clark, G. C. & Dickson, C. G. C.; *Life Histories of the South African Lycaenid Butterflies*; 1971.

Collins, M. M. & Weast, R. D.; *Wild Silk Moths of the U.S.*; Collins Radio Co, 1961.

Collins, N. M. & Morris, M. G.; *Threatened Swallowtail Butterflies of the World*; IUCN, 1985 (ISBN No. 2 88032-603-6).

Corbet, A. S. & Pendlebury, H. M.; *The Butterflies of the Malay Peninsula*; 1934.

D'Abrera, B.; *Birdwing Butterflies of the World*; Landsdowne, 1975 (ISBN 0-7018-0368-1).

D'Abrera, B.; *Butterflies of the Afrotropical Region*; Landsdowne, 1980 (ISBN 0-7018-1029-7).

D'Abrera, B.; *Butterflies of the Neotropical Region, 1*; Landsdowne, 1981 (ISBN 0-7018-1033-5).

Emmel, T. C., Minno, M. C., & Drummond, B. A.; *Florissant Butterflies, A Guide to the Fossil and Present-Day Species of Central Colorado*; Stanford. 1992 (ISBN 0–8047–1938–1).

Ehrlich, P. R.; *Butterflies Of North America*; Brown, 1961.

Ford, A.; *Audubon's Butterflies, Moths And Other Studies*; Studio Publications, 1952.

Ford, E. B.; *Butterflies*; New Naturalist Series, 1946.

Garth, J. S. & Tilden, J. W.; *California Butterflies*; 1986 (ISBN 0-520-05249-8).

Gibbons, B.; *The Fascinating World Of Butterflies & Moths*; Grange, 1997 (ISBN 1-84013-017-2).

Harris, L.; *Butterflies of Georgia*; 1972 (ISBN 0-8061-0965-3).

Higgins, L. G. & Riley, N. D.; *A Field Guide to the Butterflies and Moths of Britain and Europe*; Collins, 1970 (ISBN 0 00212028 3).

Holland, W. J.; *The Butterfly Book*; Doubleday, 1899).

Humphreys, H. N. & Westwood, J. O.; *British Butterflies & their Transformations*; Smith, 1841.

Jermyn, L.; *The Butterfly Collector's Vade Mecum*; London, 1824.

Blue Morpho (*Morpho granadensis*).

Painted Lady (*Cynthia cardui*).

Kirby, W. F.; *European Butterflies and Moths*; Cassell, 1882.

Klots, A. B.; *A Field Guide to the Butterflies of Eastern North America*; Houghton Mifflin, 1987 (ISBN 0-395-07865-2).

Lewis, H. L.; *Butterflies Of The World*; Harrap, 1974 (ISBN 0-245-52097-X).

Lisney, A. A.; *A Bibliography of British Lepidoptera 1608-1799*; 1960.

Longstaff, G. B.; *Butterfly Hunting In Many Lands*; Longmans, 1912.

Merian, M. S.; *Butterflies, Beetles and other Insects*; McGovern-Hill, 1976.

Preston-Mafham, R. & K.; *Butterflies of the World*; Blandford, 1988 (ISBN 0-7137-1884-6).

Pyle, R. M.; *The Audubon Society Field Guide to North American Butterflies*; 1986 (ISBN 0-394-51914-0).

Reichholf-Riehm, Dr. H.; *Field Guide to Butterflies and Moths of Britain and Europe*; Crowood, 1991 (ISBN 1 85223 593 4).

Riley, N. D.; *A Field Guide to the Butterflies of the West Indies*; Collins, 1975 (ISBN 0-00-219282-9).

Sbordoni, V. & Forestiero, S.; *The World of Butterflies*; Guild Publishing, 1985.

Simon, H.; *Milkweed Butterflies, Monarch, Models & Mimics*; 1969 (ISBN 0-8149-0006-2).

Smart, P.; *The Illustrated Encyclopaedia of the Butterfly World*; Hamlyn. 1978 (ISBN 0-600-31381-6).

Stratton-Porter, G.; *Moths of the Limberlost*; Hodder & Stoughton, c.1920.

Tilden, J. W.; *Butterflies Of The San Francisco Bay Region*; University Of California, 1965.

Tilden, J. W. & Smith, A. C.; *Western Butterflies (USA)*; Houghton Mifflin, 1986 (ISBN 0-395-35407-2).

Tuskes, P. M., Tuttle, J. P. & Collins, M. M.; *The Wild Silk Moths of North America*; Comstock, 1996 (ISBN 0-8014-3130-1).

Watson, A., Whalley, P., & Duckworth, W.; *The Dictionary of Butterflies and Moths in Colour*; Peerage Books, 1983 (ISBN 0 907408 62 1).